DARK EMU IN THE CLASSROOM

AF585118

SIMONE BARLOW ASHLEE HORYNIAK

DARK EMU IN THE CLASSROOM

TEACHER RESOURCES FOR HIGH SCHOOL GEOGRAPHY

BIOMES AND FOOD SECURITY
ENVIRONMENTAL CHANGE AND MANAGEMENT
BASED ON DARK EMU BY BRUCE PASCOE

First Edition published 2019, reprinted 2019, 2021
Magabala Books Aboriginal Corporation, Broome, Western Australia
Website: www.magabala.com
Email: sales@magabala.com

Magabala Books is supported by the Commonwealth Government through the Australia Council, and the State of Western Australia through the Department of Local Government, Sport and Cultural Industries. Magabala Books would like to acknowledge the generous support of the Shire of Broome, Western Australia.

ISBN: 978 1 925768 64 0

Copyright © Magabala Books Aboriginal Corporation 2019
The authors Magabala Books Aboriginal Corporation assert their moral rights.
All rights reserved. Apart from any fair dealing for the purposes of private study, research, criticism or review, as permitted under the Copyright Act, no part of this publication may be reproduced by any process whatsoever without the written consent of the Publisher.

Copying of this work by educational institutions or teachers

The purchasing educational institution and its staff, or the purchasing individual teacher, may only reproduce pages within this book in accordance with the Copyright Act 1968 (the Act) and provided the educational institution (or body that administers it) has given a remuneration notice to the Copyright Agency Limited (CAL) under the Act.

For details of the CAL license for educational institutions contact:
Copyright Agency Limited
Level 12, 66 Goulburn Street
Sydney NSW 2000
Telephone (02) 9394 7600
Facsimile (02) 9394 7601
Email memberservices@copyright.com.au

Copying of the handouts

The purchasing educational institution and its staff are permitted to make copies of the pages marked as handouts, beyond their rights under the Act, provided that:

1. The number of copies are reasonable for the teaching purposes within the purchasing institution
2. Copies are reproduced by photocopying, not by digital means, and are not stored or transmitted
3. Copies are not sold or lent
4. Every copy made clearly shows the footnote.

Consultants and reviewers

Lorraine Chaffer, Geography Education Consultant, Geography Teachers Association of New South Wales President 2017–19 (or Board member)
Judy Mraz, Director of Projects, Geography Teachers Association of Victoria

Acknowledgements

The authors and publisher are grateful to the following for permission to reproduce copyright material:
Australian Curriculum (AC) codes pp. xx and xx © Australian Curriculum, Assessment and Reporting Authority (ACARA) 2009 to present, unless otherwise indicated. This material was downloaded from the ACARA website (www.acara.edu.au) September 2018 and was not modified. The material is licensed under CC BY 4.0 (https://creativecommons.org/licenses/by/4.0/). ACARA does not endorse any product that uses ACARA material or make any representations as to the quality of such products. Any product that uses material published on this website should not be taken to be affiliated with ACARA or have the sponsorship or approval of ACARA. It is up to each person to make their own assessment of the product.

Note

At the time of printing, the Internet addresses appearing in this book were correct. Owing to the dynamic nature of the Internet, however, we cannot guarantee that all these addresses will remain correct.

Internal design and typesetting by Post Pre-Press
Cover design by John Canty

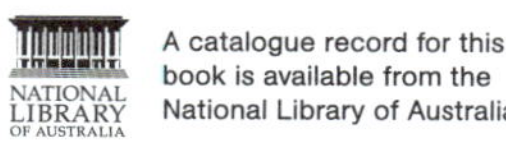

CONTENTS

DARK EMU

Dark Emu, Aboriginal Australia and the birth of agriculture (2018) is a critically acclaimed book that re-examines the culture and society of pre-colonial Aboriginal Australians. Author Bruce Pascoe presents a logical and convincing argument for the presence of pre-European Aboriginal economy and in doing so challenges the notion that Aboriginal Australians were hunter-gatherers. His call for a revision of history is compelling. Using evidence from a range of sources, including the diaries of early colonists and explorers, Pascoe encourages readers to look beyond what they may have been taught in schools or seen portrayed in mainstream media and to question the dominant historical narrative as constructed by white Australians.

Pascoe explores multiple facets of Aboriginal society to portray a thriving pre-colonial civilisation. He points to the cultivation of the yam daisy as evidence of domesticated plants, the use of fire as a tool to promote natural regeneration and control the surrounding environment, and numerous examples of fishing techniques that were established well before colonists arrived. Through these, he acknowledges a system of governance that allowed food production, slow and sustainable growth and land management.

Centred in the past, through an examination of primary source material as evidence, *Dark Emu* also relates to the present and future. Pascoe suggests that Aboriginal Australian techniques may hold the key for a sustainable future, noting kangaroo harvesting as a contemporary method of conserving land and reducing greenhouse gas emissions. He stresses the need for consultation and increased Aboriginal participation as an essential step for inter-cultural communication and prosperity for all.

Dark Emu is an important text not least because it allows the inclusion of Aboriginal perspectives in the curriculum. It presents an alternative view of the past, bringing forward the voices of those previously silenced while serving as a reminder for students that history is interpretation. Simply put, *Dark Emu* should be compulsory reading for every teacher.

ABOUT BRUCE PASCOE

M. Newton, Rummin Productions

The best-selling *Dark Emu* (2014) continues to go into reprint and won the Book of the Year and Indigenous Writer's Prize in the 2016 NSW Premier's Literary Awards. Adapted as a major new dance work by Bangarra Dance Theatre, *Dark Emu* premiered in Sydney in 2018 and toured to sold-out shows across the country.

Bruce Pascoe is a Bunurong, Tasmanian and Yuin man who lives on country, deep in the Victorian bush. His career has spanned teaching, farming, bartending, writing, working on an archaeological site, and researching Aboriginal languages.

Bruce has written more than 20 books, including short story collections, novels, historical works and books for children and young adults, including *Fog a Dox* (2012), which won the Prime Minister's Literary Award for YA Fiction in 2013. In 2017, *Mrs Whitlam* (2016) was shortlisted in the Younger Readers category in the CBCA's Book of the Year Awards.

Bruce has appeared at numerous national and international events and festivals and was featured in Indigenous filmmaker, Warwick Thornton's 2017 documentary, *We don't need a map*. In 2018, he was the recipient of the Australia Council for the Arts prestigious Lifetime Achievement Award for Literature.

A children's version of *Dark Emu* will be published by Magabala Books in 2019.

DARK EMU IN THE CLASSROOM

Dark Emu in the Classroom is a resource to assist teachers using the ideas in *Dark Emu* in their curriculum. This resource offers teachers a way to embed the Australian Curriculum's Aboriginal and Torres Strait Islander cross-cultural perspectives in the subject of Geography.

Dark Emu is drawn from the diaries and notebooks of early explorers, settlers and artists. The book provides evidence and challenges our perspectives on the life of Aboriginal and Torres Strait Islander peoples prior to European settlement.

One challenge teachers often face is in teaching cultures of which they have very little knowledge or experience. While it can be uncomfortable for non-Indigenous teachers to teach about Aboriginal and Torres Strait Islander culture, it is better to try than not attempt it at all. We think the best approach is for teachers to educate themselves as best they can, and *Dark Emu* is a fantastic place to start. Moreover, the inclusion of this text is a way to stop teaching about Aboriginal people and start including Aboriginal perspectives across a range of topics.

Dark Emu in the Classroom presents curriculum content from an Aboriginal Peoples' perspective for the topics:

- Biomes and Food Security (Vic Year 9)/ Sustainable Biomes (NSW Stage 5)
- Environmental Change and Management (Vic Year 10/NSW Stage 5)

The lessons are designed to be used individually or in a sequence. Teachers can pick and choose activities that are appropriate for their students. Differentiation options are included for less-able/ more-able students. We have also been mindful to include activities that cover the capabilities that are transferable across disciplines: ethical, personal and social, critical and creative thinking and intercultural. There are also activities with a focus on both literacy and numeracy skills.

CROSS-CURRICULUM PRIORITIES

The cross-curriculum priorities of Aboriginal and Torres Strait Islanders Histories and Cultures, and Sustainability are woven throughout the resource. *Dark Emu in the Classroom: Geography 9 and 10* provides an opportunity for Geography teachers to immerse their students in the cross-curriculum priorities through the lessons on Biomes and Food Security and Environmental Change and Management.

ABORIGINAL AND TORRES STRAIT ISLANDERS HISTORIES AND CULTURES

The following statement in the Humanities and Social Sciences learning area of the Australian Curriculum articulates how the Aboriginal and Torres Strait Islanders Histories and Cultures can be incorporated into Geography.

The diverse cultures of Aboriginal and Torres Strait Islander peoples are explored through their:

- *Long and continuous strong connections with Country/Place and their economic, cultural, spiritual and aesthetic value of place, including the idea of custodial responsibility. Students examine the influence of Aboriginal and Torres Strait Islander peoples on the environmental characteristics of Australian places, and the different ways in which places are represented.*

- *Experiences before, during and after European colonisation, including the nature of contact with other peoples, and their progress towards recognition and equality. In particular, students investigate the status and rights of Aboriginal and Torres Strait Islander peoples, past and present, including civic movements for change, the contribution of Aboriginal and Torres Strait Islander peoples to Australian society, and contemporary issues.*

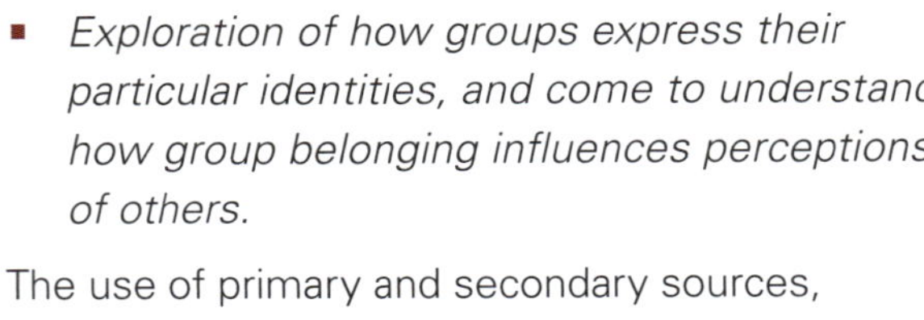

- *Exploration of how groups express their particular identities, and come to understand how group belonging influences perceptions of others.*

The use of primary and secondary sources, including oral histories, gives students opportunities to see events through multiple perspectives, and to empathise and ethically consider the investigation, preservation and conservation of sites of significance to Aboriginal and Torres Strait Islander Peoples (Source: https://www.australiancurriculum.edu.au/f-10-curriculum/cross-curriculum-priorities/aboriginal-and-torres-strait-islander-histories-and-cultures/).

SUSTAINABILITY

The following statement in the Humanities and Social Sciences learning area of the Australian Curriculum articulates how Sustainability can be incorporated into Geography.

The Australian Curriculum: Humanities and Social Sciences help students develop the ability to question, think critically, solve problems, communicate effectively, make decisions and adapt to change. Students respond to the challenges of sustainability requiring an understanding of the key historical, geographical, political, economic and societal factors involved, and how these different factors interrelate. The learning area provides content that supports the development of students' world views, particularly in relation to judgements about past social and economic systems, and access to, and use of, Earth's resources. It gives students opportunities to integrate their study of biophysical processes with investigations of the attitudinal, demographic, social, economic and political influences on human use and management of the environment. The curriculum prepares students to be informed consumers, to act in enterprising and innovative ways and to perceive business opportunities in changing local, regional and global economic environments. Students explore contemporary issues of sustainability and develop action plans and possible solutions to local, national and global issues which have social, economic and environmental perspectives. (Source: https://www.australiancurriculum.edu.au/f-10-curriculum/cross-curriculum-priorities/sustainability/).

ADVICE FOR TEACHERS

It is important to note that Bruce Pascoe does not speak for every Aboriginal and Torres Strait Islander person. While he presents a range of sources as evidence, the opinions expressed in *Dark Emu* are his own. *Dark Emu* abounds in evidence to use in the classroom.

It is also highly recommended that you connect with your local Indigenous group and invite them to talk with your students. Ideally with a focus not just on traditional practices of the past, but how they are used today in current projects.

HOW TO USE DARK EMU IN THE CLASSROOM: GEOGRAPHY 9 AND 10

Whilst we recommend reading *Dark Emu* for yourself, this teacher resource is designed so that teachers without the book, *Dark Emu*, and with little prior knowledge, can pick it up and teach. It is, however, recommended to read the synopsis from *Dark Emu* targeted at students, before starting the lesson.

The lessons follow an inquiry learning approach integrating a range of pedagogical tools.

LESSON STRUCTURE

Each lesson is structured in the same way. It starts with a 'quick-find' boxed section that includes:

- Learning intentions
- Key inquiry questions
- Key vocabulary
- Time needed to run the lesson
- Materials required

Teacher Instructions for the lesson follow. They include:

- Prior knowledge required
- Starter activity
- Main activity
- Plenary or concluding activity

At the end of the Teacher Instructions you will also find options for:

- Alternative lesson suggestions
- Differentiation for both less-able/more-able students

Reproducible Student Handouts needed for the lesson are at the end of each lesson.

FLIP THE CLASSROOM

One way to use this resource is to 'flip the classroom' by providing students with the reading/synopsis as homework and have them prepare in advance for the lesson. When it works, this allows for deeper engagement with the material and activities.

GEOGRAPHIC KNOWLEDGE AND UNDERSTANDING

The AC/NSW and Victorian codes for Geographic knowledge and understanding are provided in the Curriculum Grid on pages 10 and 11. Some lessons cover more than one understanding, allowing for rich learning.

GEOGRAPHIC SKILLS

Geographic skills such as map reading, spatial distribution analysis, and graphing, have been included in the lessons. We assume some prior knowledge and experience with the geographic skills by this stage, but some pre-teaching or scaffolding might be required depending on your students.

KEY GEOGRAPHIC CONCEPTS

The Key Geographic concepts are embedded in the lessons, particularly those of place, interconnection, environment, sustainability and change. Those relevant are listed in the Curriculum Grid.

CAPABILITIES

Capabilities are also included in the Curriculum Grid. For Victoria, codes are also used to identify the specific content descriptor relevant to the lesson.

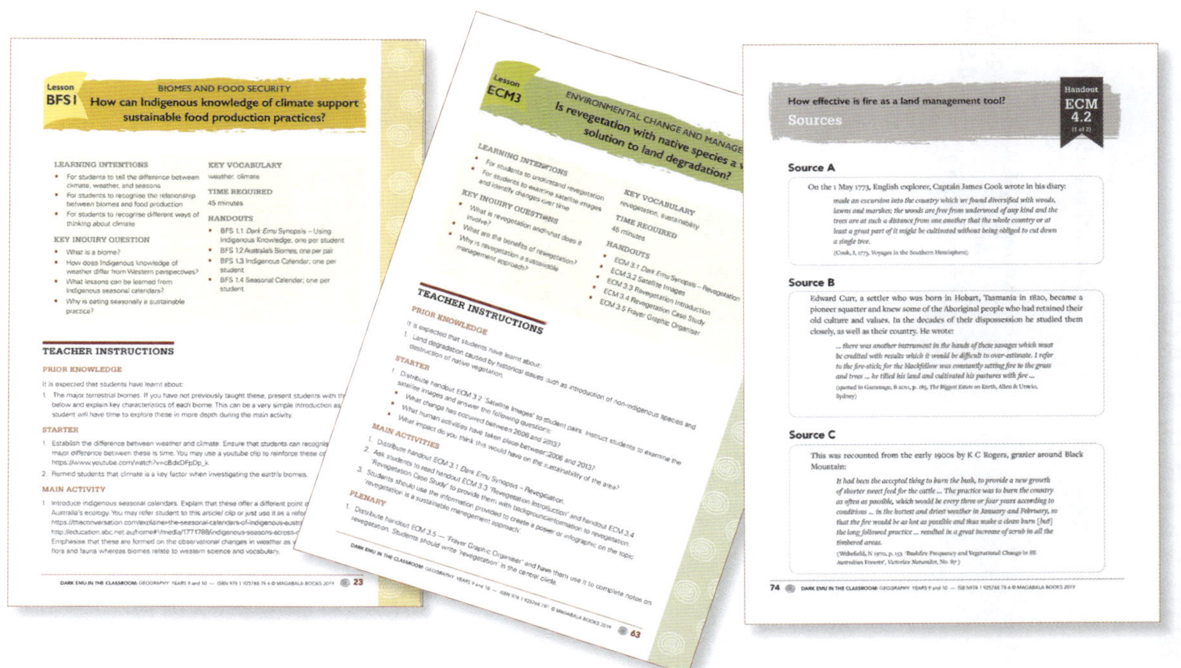

Lesson BFS1 — BIOMES AND FOOD SECURITY — How can Indigenous knowledge of climate support sustainable food production practices?

LEARNING INTENTIONS

KEY VOCABULARY

TIME REQUIRED

HANDOUTS

KEY INQUIRY QUESTION

TEACHER INSTRUCTIONS

PRIOR KNOWLEDGE

STARTER

MAIN ACTIVITY

Lesson ECM3 — ENVIRONMENTAL CHANGE AND MANAGEMENT — Is revegetation with native species a solution to land degradation?

TEACHER INSTRUCTIONS

How effective is fire as a land management tool? Sources — Handout ECM 4.2

Source A

Source B

Source C

CURRICULUM GRID YEAR 9/STAGE 5

Topic	Lesson	Title	Australian/NSW Curriculum		Victorian Curriculum		Key Geographic Concepts	Capabilities
			Knowledge and Understanding	Inquiry and Skills	Knowledge and Understanding	Concepts and Skills		
Year 9 or Year 10	Introductory activity (IA)	Were Aboriginal Australians hunter-gatherers?	ACHGK060 ACHGK071 ACHGK07	ACHGS065/074 ACHGS068/077 ACHGS070/079	VCGGK137 VCGGK138		Sustainability Environment Change	Critical and creative thinking VCCCTQ045 VCCCTM051
Biomes and Food Security (Year 9) Sustainable Biomes (Stage 5)	BFS 1	How can Indigenous knowledge of climate support sustainable practices?	ACHGK060 ACHGK061 ACHGK062	ACHGS068/077 ACHGS069/078 ACHGS067/076	VCGGK133 VCGGK134 VCGGK137		Sustainability Environment Interconnection	Ethical understanding Intercultural understanding VCECU020 VCICCB018
	BFS 2	How have Aboriginal and Torres Strait Islanders achieved food security?	ACHGK064	ACHGS067/076 ACHGS070/079	VCGGK136 VCGGK137	VCGGC128 VCGGC132	Sustainability Environment Space	
	BFS 3	How have Aboriginal and Torres Strait Islanders changed biomes to produce food?	ACHGK061	ACHGS063/072 ACHGS064/073 ACHGS065/074	VCGGC129 VCGGK136	VCGGK137	Sustainability Environment Interconnection Change	Critical and creative thinking VCCCTQ044 VCCCTQ045
	BFS 4	How can food production be managed to produce food sustainably in the future?	ACHGK064	ACHGS068/077 ACHGS070/079	VCGGK135 VCGGK137	VCGGC127	Sustainability Environment	Intercultural understanding VCICCB017
	BFS 5	What role could Indigenous strategies play in ensuring food security across Australia?	ACHGK064	ACHGS065/074 ACHGS070/079	VCGGK137 VCGGK138	VCGGC127 VCGGC130	Sustainability Environment Interconnection Change	

CURRICULUM GRID YEAR 10/STAGE 5

Topic	Lesson	Title	Australian/NSW Curriculum		Victorian Curriculum		Key Geographic Concepts	Capabilities
			Knowledge and Understanding	Skills	Knowledge and Understanding	Concepts and Skills		
Environmental Change and Management (Year 10/Stage 5)	ECM 1	How have Australian environment has been changed?	ACHGK070 ACHGK073	ACHGS064/073 ACHGS066/075 ACHGS070/079	VCGGK144 VCGGK145 VCGGK148	VCGGC127	Sustainability Environment Interconnection Change Place	Intercultural understanding VCICCB017
	ECM 2	Does the consumption of kangaroo meat have a future in Australia?	ACHGK071 ACHGK072	ACHGS064/073 ACHGS068/077	VCGGK146 VCGGK148		Sustainability Environment	Critical and creative thinking VCCCTM053 Personal and social VCPSCSO047 VCPSCSO050
	ECM 3	Is revegetation using native species a viable solution to land degradation?	ACHGK074 ACHGK075	ACHGS064/073 ACHGS065/074 ACHGS070/079	VCGGK145 VCGGK148		Sustainability Environment Interconnection Place	
	ECM 4	How effective is fire as a land management tool?	ACHGK074 ACHGK075	ACHGS064/073 ACHGS065/074 ACHGS070/079	VCGGK146 VCGGK147 VCGGK148	VCGGC130	Sustainability Environment Change	Personal and social capability VCPSCSE045
	ECM 5	Should Australia diversify its crops?	ACHGS064/073 ACHGS066/075 ACHGS070/079	ACHGS064/073 ACHGS066/075 ACHGS070/079	VCGGK144 VCGGK145 VCGGK148	VCGGC132	Sustainability Environment Change Interconnection Space	
	ECM 6	How should Australia manage its land degradation issues?	ACHGK074 ACHGK075	ACHGS064/073 ACHGS068/077 ACHGS067/076	VCGGK146 VCGGK148 VCGGK149		Sustainability Environment	Critical and creative thinking VCCCTM051 VCCCTM053
Year 9 or Year 10	Reflection activity (RA)	Where to next?	ACHGK075	ACHGS068/077 ACHGS070/079 ACHGS071/080	VCGGK138	VCGGC130		Ethical understanding Intercultural understanding VCECU020 VCICCD019

Lesson IA

INTRODUCTORY ACTIVITY

Were Aboriginal Australians hunter-gatherers?

LEARNING INTENTIONS

- For students to explore whether Aboriginal Australians were **hunter-gatherers**
- For student to challenge their previously held assumptions
- For students to analyse a range of sources and draw a conclusion

KEY INQUIRY QUESTION

- What does the term hunter-gatherer imply?
- What is meant by the term '**agriculture**'?
- Were Aboriginal Australians hunter-gatherers?

KEY VOCABULARY

hunter-gatherer, *terra nullius*, agriculture

TIME REQUIRED

90 minutes

HANDOUTS

- IA.1 *Dark Emu* Synopsis – Hunter-gatherers; one per student
- IA.2: Sources for analysis (Sets A – E); one set per group with copies for each student
- IA.3: Graphic organiser; one per student

TEACHER INSTRUCTIONS

PRIOR KNOWLEDGE

No prior knowledge is required for this lesson. Complete this at a year 9 or 10 level to begin a discussion of Aboriginal and Torres Strait Islander peoples.

STARTER

1. Play 'odd one out'. Begin by writing the following three statements on the board:
   a. Aboriginal Australians were hunter-gatherers.
   b. Aboriginal Australians grew their own food.
   c. Aboriginal Australians built the oldest human structure on earth.
2. Ask students to decide which one they think is false. Conduct a class vote on which they think is false. Ask a couple of students to justify their position.
3. Do not provide an answer to students, leave the answers on the board and tell them you will return to this at the end of the lesson.

MAIN ACTIVITY

1. Distribute handout IA.1 *Dark Emu* Synopsis — Hunter-gatherers. Read together as a class.
2. Distribute handout IA.3 Graphic Organiser
3. Conduct a Jigsaw activity.
   a. Arrange students into five groups. Give each group a set of sources (A, B, C, D or E). They should read through the sources and discuss as a group. Ask students to complete the relevant row in the graphic organiser.

   b. Create new groups, with one member from each original group (one student from A, B, C, D and E). Students share their findings and complete the graphic organiser.
4. Ask students to synthesise their understanding by creating a poster or infographic answering the question, 'Were Aboriginal Australians hunter-gatherers?'

PLENARY

1. Return to that 'odd one out' from the beginning of the lesson. Ask students to reflect on whether their answer has changed.
2. Conduct a class discussion around the information learnt today:
   a. Were they surprised by any of the information?
   b. Is the information reliable? You can link back to the idea that multiple sources were consulted, ideas corroborated, and the notion that the white colonists and farmers had little to gain from recording this information.
   c. Why don't we already know this? You can link in the ideas of this truth being inconvenient, that it cancels out the very foundation of **colonisation** on '**Terra Nullius**', and the implications of accepting this perspective.

DIFFERENTIATION

For less-able students:

- Pair up these students with a strong partner. Encourage them to join in the discussion to ensure they don't just copy down the answers.

For more-able students:

- Provide students with the Introduction and Chapter 1 of *Dark Emu*.
- Have students research and find additional evidence to support the notion that Aboriginal Australians were not hunter-gatherers.
- Have students write 3–5 questions for Bruce Pascoe based on the reading.

SUGGESTED ADAPTATIONS

- You could present students with the synopsis and one or two sources, and then have them research to find more evidence that supports the theory.

Dark Emu Synopsis

Were Aboriginal Australians hunter-gatherers?

Hunter-gatherers

Lesson **IA.1**

The common narrative taught in Australian schools is that Aboriginal Australians were **hunter-gatherers**, that they foraged and lived off what they could find. *Dark Emu*, by Bruce Pascoe, brings together evidence from a vast array of people – colonists, settlers, explorers, anthropologists, Aboriginal elders, historians and authors – to contradict this assumption. This research suggests they had systems of **agriculture**, **aquaculture**, housing, food storage and land management, inconsistent with hunter-gatherer societies.

First, it is important to examine a definition of agriculture. Pascoe references Australian historian Rupert Gerritsen's theories to refer to five signifiers of agriculture: selection of seed, preparation of the soil, **harvest** of the crop, storage of surpluses, and large populations and permanent housing.

Hunter-gatherers forage and hunt for food. They don't use agricultural methods or build permanent dwellings. But this is exactly what the Australian Aboriginals did. Analysis of early colonists and explorers reveal Aboriginals planted, **irrigated** and **cultivated** seeds, and also built structures to store surplus grain and food. They built dams and wells, had elaborate ceremonies and purposefully changed the landscape.

> *While we continue to think of Aboriginal people having no construction skills it is easier to dismiss Aboriginal attachment to land. Moreover, the insistence on using the hunter-gatherer label is prejudicial to the rights of Aboriginal people to land.*
> (Pascoe 2018, *Dark Emu*, p.144)

One question Pascoe repeatedly raises is why Australians don't already know this? The prejudice against Aboriginals began long before current day; Australia is founded on it. From the beginning, Europeans considered themselves superior; they believed non-Western cultures to be uncivilised. The British also looked to **colonise** – to replace the existing civilisation with their own, and to profit from the land's resources. They dismissed difference and did not take the time to examine the Aboriginal and Torres Strait Islander ways of life. The colonists ignored Aboriginal methods and brought their own, which were poorly suited to the landscape.

Source: Adapted from Pascoe, 2018, *Dark Emu*: Black Seeds: agriculture or accident?, pp.13, 144

Were Aboriginal Australians hunter-gatherers?

Sources for Analysis

Read each of the sources and complete the graphic organiser in handout 2.

Set A

Pastoralist (farmer) James Dawson, who worked alongside the Kirrae Wurrung people of the Western District and published a book recording Aboriginal languages and customs, is quoted as saying:

> *Lake Boloke [Bolac] is the most celebrated place in the Western District for the fine quality and abundance of its eels; and, when the autumn rains induce these fish to leave the lake and to go down the river to the sea, the Aborigines gather there from great distances. Each tribe has allotted to it a portion of the stream and the usual strong barrier is built by each family with the eel basket in the opening.*
>
> (Morieson, J, 'Aboriginal Stone Arrangement in Victoria', Unpublished paper, Australian Centre, University of Melbourne, 1994, in Pascoe 2018, *Dark Emu* p. 78)

Early photo of the Brewarrina fish traps. Ref 85/1286–722. Tyrrell Collection, Powerhouse Museum, Sydney

> *The traps were also designed to allow the passage of breeding stock to pass through so that the upstream fisheries could gain a share. Particular ponds in the system were managed and used by particular families — but those families had responsibilities for the secure provision of fish to the families and systems upstream and downstream from their location.*
>
> (Pascoe 2018, Dark Emu p. 75)

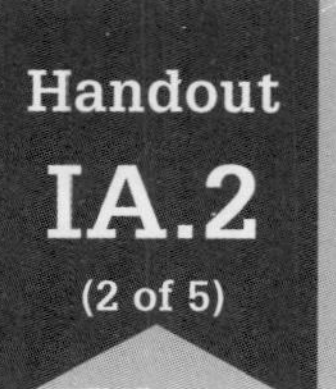

Set B

Alfred Howitt, Gippsland police officer and amateur anthropologist, was part of a search party looking for Burke and Wills. He noted:

> *Near Lake Lipson, one of my party, found about two bushels contained in a grass case daubed with mud. It looked like a small clay coffin and was concealed ... the munyoura [yam daisy] bower tastes like linseed-meal, and is by no means unpleasant when baked in ashes and eaten hot.*
>
> (Howitt in Smyth, R B 1878, *The Aborigines of Victoria and the Riverina*, John Ferres, Gvt Printer, quoted in Pascoe 2018, p. 148.)

RG Kimber, contemporary researcher and ethnographer, compiled evidence from Central Australia. He worked with Walter Smith, cameleer and bush worker. Smith shared this:

> *The chuck a bit there. Not much you know, wouldn't be a handful. [They] chuck a little bit, spread it you see – one seed there, one seed there, ... course they chuck a little bit of dirt on, not too much though, and soon as the first rain comes ... it will grow then.*
>
> (Kimber, R G 1984, *Resource use and management in central Australia*, Australian Aboriginal Studies, Canberra, p. 16 in Pascoe 2018, p. 29.)

Alice Duncan-Kemp grew up on a sheep station in Queensland, stated this in 1910:

> *From their woven dilly bags the gins sprinkled seed food over the ground ... Katoora or barley grass seed lay in little hillocks, already swelling and creeping to repeated applications of water which the gins [Aboriginal women] poured on them to make 'wunjee aal the same walkabout (grass to grow).'*
>
> (Duncan-Kemp, A 1934, *Our Sandhill Country*, Angus and Robertson, Sydney, in Pascoe 2018, p. 31.)

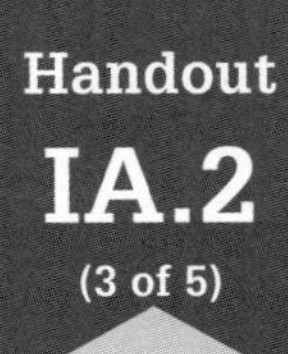

Set C

Colonist Isaac Batey, whose book about the **colonisation** of Melbourne was based on the stories of his father who arrived in Australia in 1841, noted:

> *... the soil is rich in basaltic clay, evidently well fitted for the production of myrnongs [yam daisy]. On the spot are numerous mounds with short spaces between each, and as all these are at right angles to the ridges slope it is conclusive evidence that they were the work of human hands extending over a long series of years.*
>
> (Batey, quoted in Frankel, D 1982, 'An Account of Aboriginal Use of the Yam Daisy', *The Artefact*, vol. 7 (1–2): 43–45, quoted in Pascoe 2018, *Dark Emu* p. 22.)

Major Thomas Mitchell (1792–1855) was an explorer and surveyor. He records:

> *We crossed some patches of dry swamp where the clods had been extensively turned up by the natives ... These clods were so very large and hard that we were obliged to throw them aside, and clear the way for our carts to pass. The whole resembled ground broken with a hoe ... There might be about two acres in the patch we crossed and we perceived at a distance other portions of the ground in a similar state.*
>
> (Mitchell, T L 1848, *Journal of an Expedition into the Interior of Tropical Australia*, Greenwood Press, New York 1969, quoted in Pascoe 2018, *Dark Emu* p. 25.)

Scientists from Charles Darwin University stated this on ABC Radio's rural report in October 2012:

> *Native Australian rice has been harvested and consumed by Indigenous people for thousands of years (and) may have the potential to underpin a wild rice enterprise as a 'bush tucker', 'novelty' or gourmet product (either as flour or grains) for the tourism and niche gourmet markets.*
>
> (Wurm, P et al 2012, 'Australian Native Rice: A new sustainable wild food enterprise', Research Institute for the Environment and Livelihoods, Rural Industries Research and Development Corporation, Research Project No. PRJ000347/Publication No. 10/175, quoted in Pascoe 2018, *Dark Emu* pp. 44–5.)

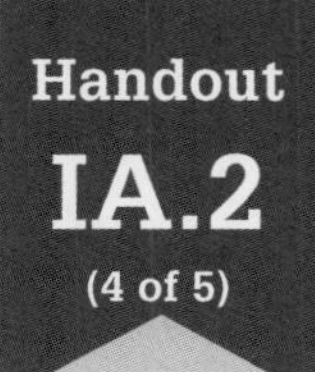

Set D

Well known explorer Charles Sturt traversed the continent starting in 1844. He recorded his travels in diaries:

> [The houses] *were made of strong boughs fixed in a circle in the ground, so as to meet in a common centre; on these there was ... a thick seam of grass and leaves and over this a compact coating of clay. They were from eight to ten feet in diameter, and about four and a half feet high, the opening in them not being larger than to allow a man to creep in. These huts also faced north-west, and each one had a smaller one attached.*
>
> (Sturt, C 1833, *Two Expeditions into the Interior of Southern Australia*, Vol. 1, p. 298, Vol. 2, p. 140, quoted in Pascoe 2018, *Dark Emu* p. 106.)

Major Thomas Mitchell (1792–1855), an explorer and surveyor, wrote about his expeditions into the interior of eastern Australia:

> *In crossing one hollow we passed among the huts of a native tribe. They were tastefully distributed amongst drooping acacias and casuarinae; ... some were isolated under the deeper shades of casuarinae; while others were placed more socially, three or four together. Each hut was semicircular, or circular, the roof conical, and from one side a flat roof stood forward like a portico, supported by two sticks ... and they were covered ... by sheets of bark, but with a variety of materials such as reeds, grass and boughs. The interior of each looked clean, and to use passing in the rain, gave some idea, not only of shelter, but even of comfort and happiness ...*
>
> (Mitchell, T L 1839, *Three Expeditions into the Interior of Eastern Australia* Vol. 1, pp. 76–7, T and W Boone, London, quoted in Pascoe 2018, *Dark Emu* pp. 108–9)

Pointed dome house. Henry Mosby (1859–1933) Mobsby, Henry William, 1859-1933 [Three children outside Meriam house, Torres Strait Islands, nd . Henry William Mobsby Collection, UQFL181, Box 2, Folder 1, photo 69.

Were Aboriginal Australians hunter-gatherers?

Sources for Analysis

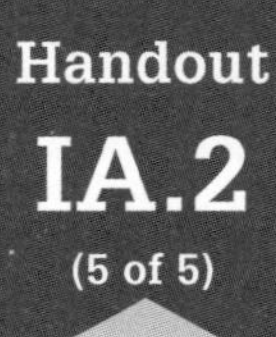

Set E

Major Thomas Mitchell (1792–1855) was an explorer and surveyor. He records:

> *The seed is made by the natives into a kind of paste or bread. Dry heaps of this grass, that has been pulled expressly for this purpose of gathering the seed, lay along our path for many miles. I counted nine miles along the river, in which we rode through this grass only, reaching to our saddle-girths, and the same grass seemed to grow back from the river, at least as far as the eye could reach through a very open forest.*
>
> (Mitchell, T L 1848, *Journal of an Expedition into the Interior of Tropical Australia*, Greenwood Press, New York, 1969, p. 90, quoted in Pascoe 2018, *Dark Emu*, p. 15.)

Well-known explorer Charles Sturt traversed the continent starting in 1844. He recorded his travels in diaries:

> *22 feet deep and 8 feet deep broad at the top. There was a landing place ... and a recess had been made to hold the water ... Paths led from this spot to almost every point of the compass, and in walking along one came to a village consisting of nineteen huts ... Troughs and stones for grinding seed were lying about ... The fact of there being so large a well at this point (a work that must have required the united labour of a powerful tribe to complete) assured us that this distant part of the interior ... was not without inhabitants.*
>
> (Sturt, C 1849, *Narrative of an Expedition into Central Australia*, T & W Boone, p. 90, quoted in Pascoe 2018, *Dark Emu*, p. 47–8.)

Wells at Kooyoora National Park, near Bendigo, Victoria
(Lyn Harwood in Pascoe 2018, *Dark Emu*, p. 48.)

Were Aboriginal Australians hunter-gatherers?

Graphic Organiser

Handout **IA.3**

Source	What do these sources tell us about Aboriginal Australians?	What evidence is presented to support the provided definition of agriculture?	What evidence of sustainability is evident?	Are these sources reliable? Why/why not?
Set A				
Set B				
Set C				
Set D				
Set E				

NOTES

Biomes and Food Security

YEAR 9 | STAGE 5

Lesson
BFS I

BIOMES AND FOOD SECURITY

How can Indigenous knowledge of climate support sustainable food production practices?

LEARNING INTENTIONS

- For students to tell the difference between **climate**, **weather**, and seasons
- For students to recognise the relationship between **biome**s and food production
- For students to recognise different ways of thinking about climate

KEY INQUIRY QUESTION

- What is a **biome**?
- How does Indigenous knowledge of weather differ from Western perspectives?
- What lessons can be learned from Indigenous seasonal calendars?
- Why is eating seasonally a sustainable practice?

KEY VOCABULARY

weather, climate

TIME REQUIRED

45 minutes

HANDOUTS

- BFS 1.1 *Dark Emu* Synopsis – Using Indigenous Knowledge; one per student
- BFS 1.2 Australia's Biomes; one per pair
- BFS 1.3 Indigenous Calendar; one per student
- BFS 1.4 Seasonal Calendar; one per student

TEACHER INSTRUCTIONS

PRIOR KNOWLEDGE

It is expected that students have learnt about:

1. The major **terrestrial biomes**. If you have not previously taught these, present students with the map on page 28 and explain key characteristics of each biome. This can be a very simple introduction as the student will have time to explore these in more depth during the main activity.

STARTER

1. Establish the difference between weather and **climate**. Ensure that students can recognise that the major difference between these is time. You may use a YouTube clip to reinforce these concepts: https://www.youtube.com/watch?v=cBdxDFpDp_k.
2. Remind students that climate is a key factor when investigating the earth's biomes.

MAIN ACTIVITY

1. Introduce Indigenous seasonal calendars. Explain that these offer a different point of view on Australia's ecology. You may refer students to this article/clip or just use it as a reference point: https://theconversation.com/explainer-the-seasonal-calendars-of-indigenous-australia-88471 or http://education.abc.net.au/home#!/media/1771788/indigenous-seasons-across-northern-australia. Emphasise that these are formed on the observational changes in weather as well as changes in flora and fauna whereas biomes relate to Western science and vocabulary.

2. Distribute handout BFS 1.2 'Indigenous Calendar Analysis' to students and direct them to the Indigenous Seasonal Calendars on the Bureau of Meteorology website: http://www.bom.gov.au/iwk/?ref=ftr. Students should select 2–3 calendars to explore in more detail. They should complete the grid supplementing their understanding of the biome with their own research. You may ask students to locate the group on the AIATSIS map at https://aiatsis.gov.au/explore/articles/aiatsis-map-indigenous-australia of this resource which would support comparison with the handout 'Australia's biomes'.
3. Tell students that for each place explored they should look at a **climate** graph of the region to compare with the Indigenous seasonal calendar.

PLENARY

1. Ask students to consider how useful the concept of seasons is to their lives. Ask them to consider the different foods they eat or the activities they undertake at different times of the year.
2. Distribute handout BFS 1.3 'Seasonal Calendar' and ask students to complete their own personal calendar on the template provided.
3. Distribute handout BFS 1.1 *Dark Emu* Synopsis – Using Indigenous Knowledge; and have students consider this before discussing the following questions with a partner:
   a. How do the Indigenous seasonal calendars provide insight into each biome?
   b. What are the strengths and weaknesses of the different ways of categorising climate?
   c. What have you eaten in the last week? Is this food seasonal?
   d. Much of what Australians eat is transported from across the country or imported from overseas. In light of this, how might this different understanding of seasons influence food production and consumption?

DIFFERENTIATION

For less-able students:

- Use a simpler video clip: https://www.youtube.com/watch?v=YbAWny7FV3w
- The Gulumoerrgin (Larrakia) seasonal calendar is available in an online interactive (http://www.larrakia.csiro.au/#/calendar/dalay) which should suit kinaesthetic learners. They can focus on fewer locations to analyse.

For more-able students:

- More closely explore the relationship between latitude and climate (biomes) and the tilt of the earth and seasons.
- Blog post: https://blog.csiro.au/naidoc-week-calendars-and-moving-feasts/

SUGGESTED ADAPTATIONS

- Ask your students to pre-read the following article: https://www.theguardian.com/lifeandstyle/wordofmouth/2014/aug/12/seasonal-eating-vegetables-uk-does-it-matter
- Seasonal calendars are also published by the CSIRO (https://www.csiro.au/en/Research/Environment/Land-management/Indigenous/Indigenous-calendars)
- This resource provides a great video overview of seasons as understood by the Yolngu people of Ramingining in northern Central Arnhem Land http://www.12canoes.com.au/

Dark Emu Synopsis

How can Indigenous knowledge of climate support sustainable food production practices?

Using Indigenous Knowledge

Handout
BFS
1.1

The history of Australia, though widely accepted across the nation, is one that has been filtered through European experiences. When colonists arrived, they described the landscape as a site for profit, ignoring the existing practices and methods, perhaps because they knew they were there to replace it. Thus, through more than two centuries since Europeans colonised this land, Aboriginal and Torres Strait Islander culture and knowledge has been grossly undervalued.

There is evidence of constructions that seem to have been created to predict the solstice, knowledge that would have assisted in the **cultivation** of plants, suggesting a thorough understanding of **climate** on food production.

Research suggests that Aboriginal and Torres Strait Islander peoples had an agricultural economy in which seeds were propagated, irrigated, harvested, stored and traded across regions. In fact, early records so clearly illustrate grain harvests that an Aboriginal grain belt would likely have stretched across the country through central regions. This is in stark contrast to the contemporary grain belt which is clustered in Western Australia and the South-East. Further to this, it was seen that areas beyond the high rainfall zones in coastal regions used grain as the **staple crop** while in wetter areas yam production took over.

There is much evidence that Aboriginals were intervening in the productivity of the country and what they learnt during that process over many thousands of years will be useful to us today.

Source: Adapted from Pascoe 2018, *Dark Emu*, pp.1–4, 27–29, 52–3

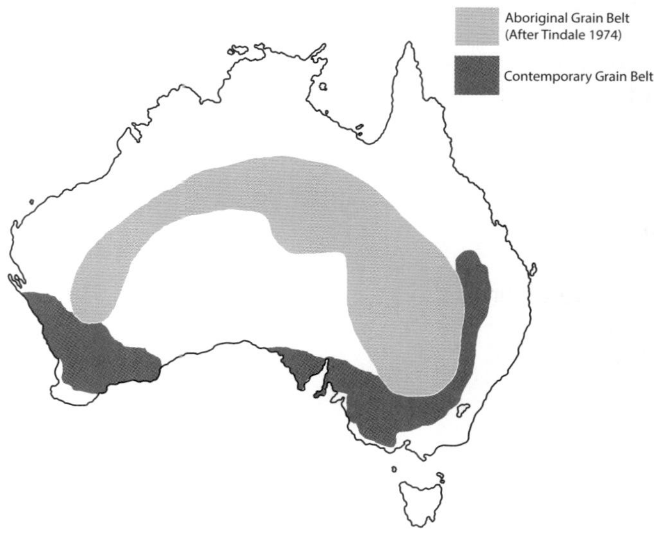

Aboriginal grain belt based on research compiled by Norman Tindale 1974 shows the extent of the harvest compared to the current Australian grain belt.

Handout

BFS 1.2

How can Indigenous knowledge of climate support sustainable food production practices?

Australia's Biomes

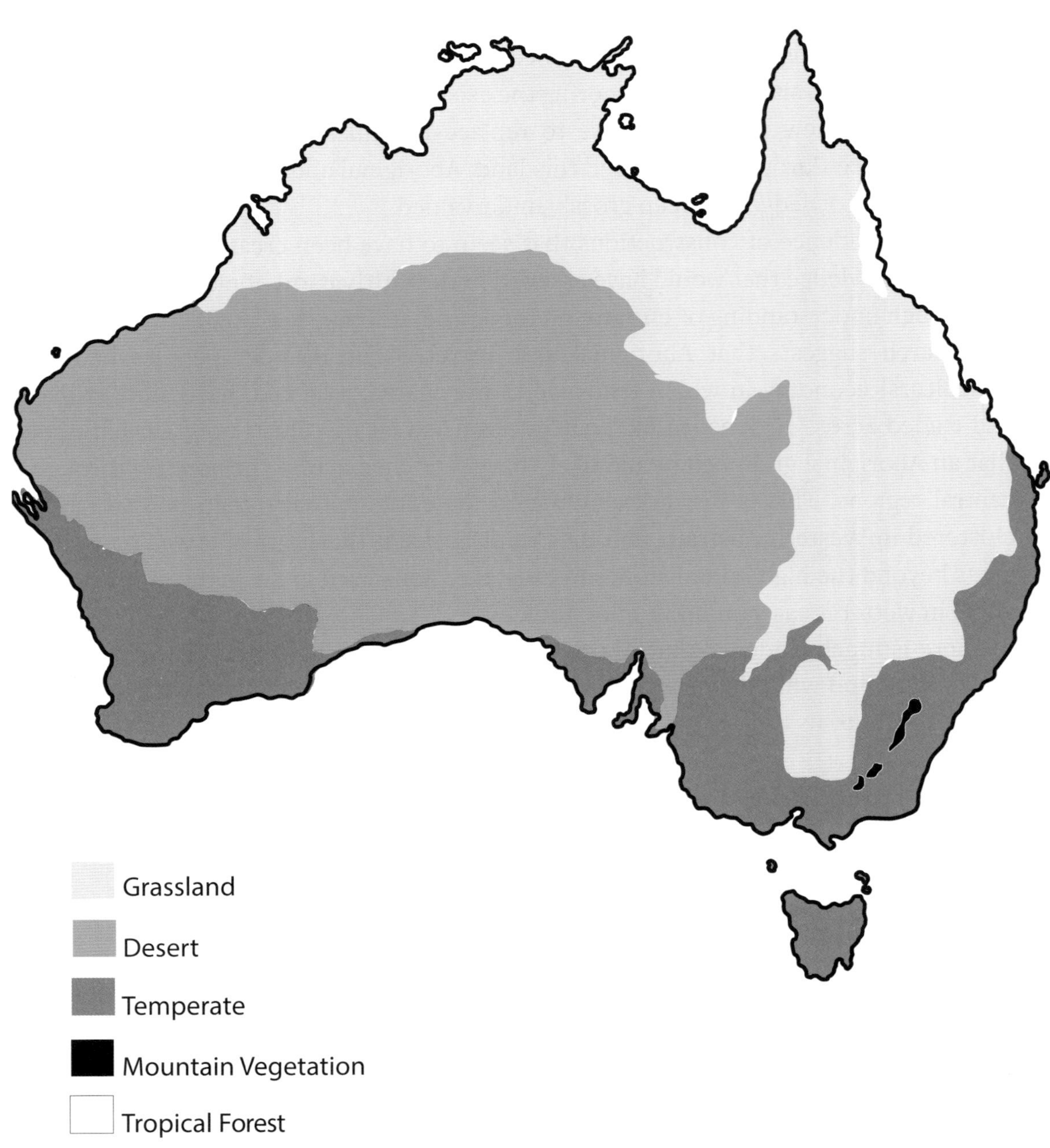

Handout **BFS 1.3**

How can Indigenous knowledge of climate support sustainable food production practices?

Indigenous Calendar Analysis

Use the BOM Indigenous Seasonal Calendars (http://www.bom.gov.au/iwk/index.shtml) as well as your own research to fill in the grid below.

Indigenous language group	Seasons experienced (climate characteristics)	Food available	Biome (climate characteristics)	Food produced in this region

1. How do the Indigenous Seasonal Calendars provide insight into each biome?

___

___

2. What are the strengths and weaknesses of the different ways (Western or Indigenous) of categorising **climate**?

___

___

3. How might this different understanding of seasons influence food production and consumption?

___

___

Handout

BFS 1.4

How can Indigenous knowledge of climate support sustainable food production practices?

Seasonal Calendar

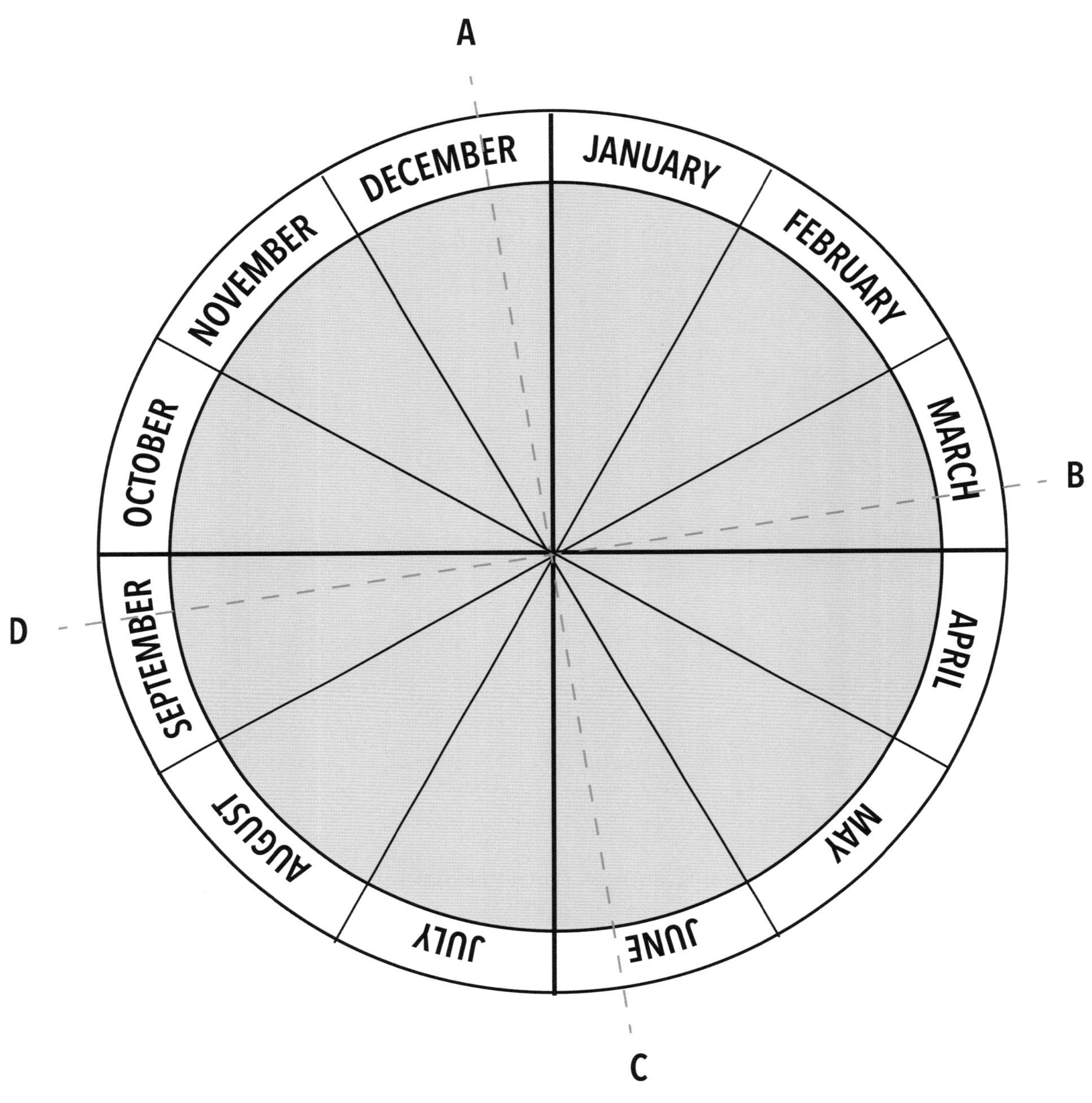

A Summer Solstice – 22 December

B Autumn Equinox – 23 March

C Winter Solstice – 22 June

D Spring Equinox – 22 September

Lesson **BFS2**

BIOMES AND FOOD SECURITY

How did Aboriginal and Torres Strait Islander Peoples achieve food security?

LEARNING INTENTIONS

- For students to explore the **cultivation** of the yam daisy
- For students to learn and apply the PQE method to analyse **spatial distribution**

KEY INQUIRY QUESTIONS

- What is the yam daisy?
- Where does the yam daisy grow?

KEY VOCABULARY

food security, food insecurity, tuber, cultivation, spatial distribution

TIME REQUIRED

45 minutes approximately

HANDOUTS

- BFS 2.1 *Dark Emu* Synopsis – Yam Daisy; one per student
- BFS 2.2 Prediction; one per pair
- BFS 2.3 Spatial Distribution of the Yam Daisy; one per student

TEACHER INSTRUCTIONS

PRIOR KNOWLEDGE

It is expected that students have learnt about:

1. Key determiners of **food security** – access, availability, appropriate use and stability over time.
2. Space as a key geographical concept.

STARTER

1. Distribute handout BFS 2.2 'Prediction'; one between two is sufficient. Ask students to talk to their partner and make a prediction of what the lesson will be about.

MAIN ACTIVITY

1. Distribute handout BFS 2.1 *Dark Emu* Synopsis – Yam Daisy. Ask students to respond by writing down one fact they found interesting and sharing this with a partner. You may wish to refer to the AIATSIS language groups map at https://aiatsis.gov.au/explore/articles/aiatsis-map-indigenous-australia to support student understanding of the Wathaurong people.
2. Guide students in an analysis of the spatial distribution of yam daisy in Australia, i.e:
   a. Direct students to the Australasian Virtual Herbarium at http://avh.chah.org.au/.
   b. Conduct a quick search of *Microseris lanceolata.*
   c. Ensure students refine the location to Australia in the left-hand panel.
   d. Have students conduct an analysis of the spatial distribution of the recorded occurrence of yam daisy in Australia using the PQE method handout BFS 2.3 'Spatial Distribution of the Yam Daisy', For example:

      P: The occurrence of *Microseris lanceolata* is clustered along the south-eastern periphery of mainland Australia.

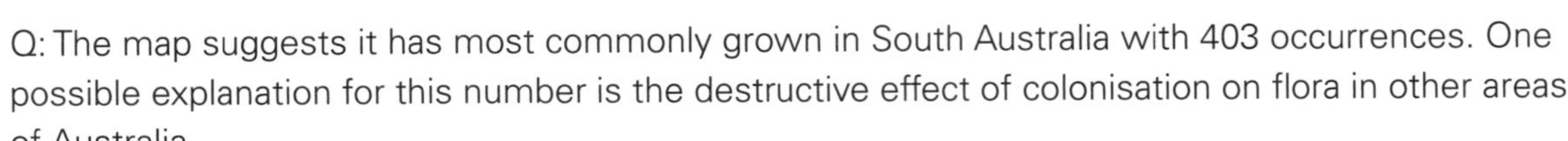

Q: The map suggests it has most commonly grown in South Australia with 403 occurrences. One possible explanation for this number is the destructive effect of colonisation on flora in other areas of Australia.

E: Though more sparse, occurrence is also randomly arranged through NSW and densely arranged in Tasmania.

e. When assisting students with quantification, you can guide them to refine their search to highlight their pattern which will provide a number of occurrences.

f. Collate possible explanations for the spatial distribution of the yam daisy.

You may wish to collect this analysis response as a piece of formative assessment.

3. Ask students to consider the determiners of **food security** and explain to a partner how the yam daisy conforms to this framework.

PLENARY

1. Distribute the article and watch the video available at https://www.sbs.com.au/food/article/2018/02/27/native-superfood-8-times-nutritious-potato-and-tastes-sweet-coconut.
2. Ask students the following discussion questions:
   a. Do you think this could mark a shift in a resurgence of the yam daisy?
   b. How could this help Australia's **food security** in the future?

DIFFERENTIATION

For less-able students:

- The *Dark Emu* Synopsis could also be made available as a closed activity.
- Complete the spatial distribution analysis as a table rather than a paragraph response or provide sentence starters.
- Ask students to annotate the parts of the yam daisy to familiarise themselves with the plant.

For more-able students:

- Read the article 'Native Knowledge: What Ecologists Are Learning from Indigenous People' available via https://e360.yale.edu/features/native-knowledge-what-ecologists-are-learning-from-indigenous-people.
- Read about Indigenous risk of **food insecurity** at https://aifs.gov.au/cfca/publications/food-insecurity-australia-what-it-who-experiences-it-and-how-can-child. Ask students to respond to the question, what example might the yam daisy highlight in fostering food security in Indigenous communities?

  Consult the National Aboriginal and Torres Strait Islander Nutrition Strategy and Action Plan, 2000–2010 via http://webarchive.nla.gov.au/gov/20140212072009/http://www.health.gov.au/internet/main/publishing.nsf/Content/health-pubhlth-strateg-food-nphp.htm. What aspects of food insecurity have been experienced by Aboriginal people? How did **colonisation** interrupt ATSI **food security**?

Dark Emu Synopsis

Handout **BFS 2.1**

How did Aboriginal and Torres Strait Islander Peoples achieve food security?

Yam Daisy

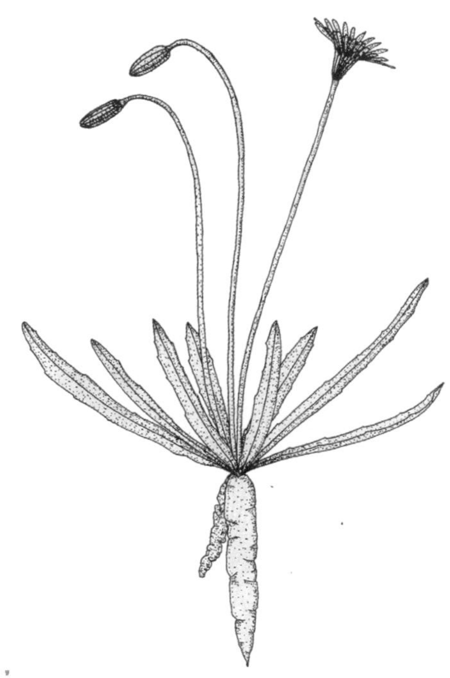

The yam daisy, also known as **murnong**, is a vegetable native to Australia. Much like a small sweet potato, it has leaves and flowers above ground, and a **tuber**, which is edible, grows below the soil. The yam daisy was a staple food of the **Wathaurong** tribe in Victoria and holds significance for the **Dhurga** in New South Wales.

The **cultivation** of the yam daisy was widespread across Australia's South-Eastern regions. Colonists noted extensive fields of murnong at the time of their arrival as evidenced in their writing and pictures. Archeologist Emeritus Professor David Frankel has noted that early explorers could identify a form of **terracing** that colonists assumed would endure for years. Here Aboriginal Australian soil management techniques such as **aeration** could sustain or increase the food supply.

As with many native species, however, this practice was disrupted by the arrival of white colonists. It was not long before they too could identify the impacts of their imposed practices. Isaac Batey noted in 1846 that the plant had become hard to find. He points to the domestication of **hard-hooved** livestock being put out to **pasture** on the **grasslands** where the tubers grew. Moreover, he notes 'another factor of destruction in the soil becoming hardened with the continuous trampling' of these animals. Once the soil is hardened, it compacts and rainwater is not absorbed, causing rivers to flood and a new agricultural problem to arise. Thus, the European theory of farming caused the principal form of sustenance to be decimated.

It is suggested that Australians continue to experience the consequences of ignoring Aboriginal methods of soil and land management. The yam daisy was once a crucial plant in Australia and, as the population continues to grow and **climate** change remains a barrier to food security, its current value must be considered.

Source: Adapted from Pascoe, B 2018, *Dark Emu*, pp.13–67

Handout
BFS 2.2

How did Aboriginal and Torres Strait Islander Peoples achieve food security?

Prediction

Examine the images below. Working with a partner, make a prediction about the focus of today's lesson and how you think it fits into the study of food security.

Yam diggers at Indented Head, Victoria. Illustration by JH Wedge, 'J.H.W. Native women getting tam bourn roots 27 August 1835'. From the *Todd Journal Andrew (alias William) Todd John Batman's recorder and his Indented Head journal 1985.* La Trobe section, State Library of Victoria, p. 70

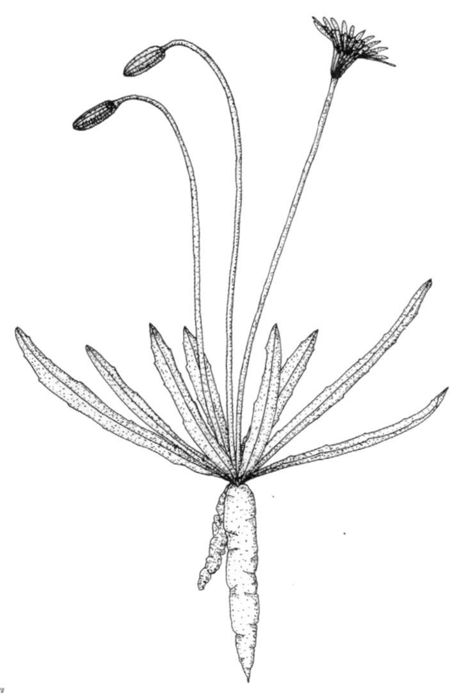

The Yam Daisy including the tuber which grows underground. Illustration by John Conran, University of Adelaide

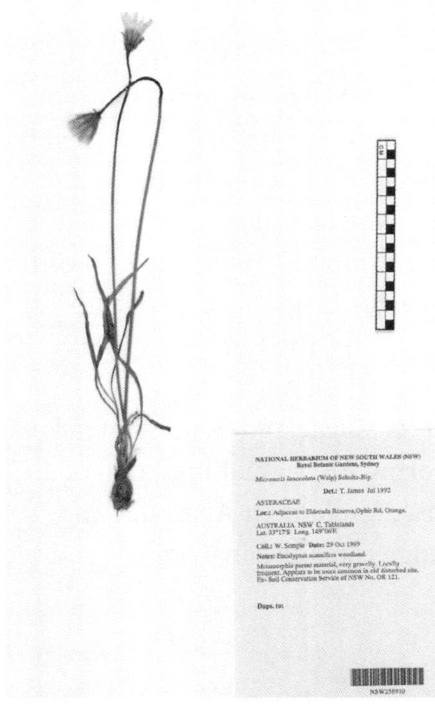

Australasian Virtual Herbarium sheet of the flower of the Microseris Lanceolata

How did Aboriginal and Torres Strait Islander Peoples achieve food security?

Spatial Distribution of the Yam Daisy

Handout BFS 2.3 (1 of 2)

Instructions

1. Access the Australasian Virtual Herbarium online at http://avh.chah.org.au/.
2. Conduct a quick search of Microseris lanceolata, the scientific name for the yam daisy.
3. Refine the country to Australia by clicking on location in the left-hand panel.
4. Use this worksheet to make some observations, then write a paragraph about the spatial distribution of the reported occurrence of yam daisy in Australia using PQE.

Identifying spatial distribution

Geographers look for trends in geographical data to further understand the world around us. In order to analyse how things are spread out on a map, geographers can use the PQE method:

Pattern: What pattern can you identify in the way the data is arranged? Does it all seem close together (densely arranged) or far apart (sparsely arranged)?

When looking at where things are located, it's important to notice the formation and density of how the data is arranged. Look for one of the following patterns:

Dispersed — Linear — Radial — Random — Clustered

Quantification: How might you refine your description of the pattern? Make reference to a number in your response.

Exception: Can you identify an example in your geographical data that doesn't fit into the pattern?

Dispersed	Linear	Radial	Random	Clustered
A dispersed pattern is when the feature is *spread evenly* over the map. The feature covers the map relatively evenly.	A linear pattern *follows a line* – it does not have to be perfectly straight, it may curve. This will often be along roads, rivers or borders.	A radial pattern appears similiar to the spokes of a wheel – spreading out or *radiating out from a central point.*	A random pattern shows *no link/shape/ connection* between the features in any way. Some may be close together, others far apart.	A clustered pattern is demostrated by *features grouped together around a point.* There may be several clusters on a map. These will often be around towns, cities or other major attractions.

How did Aboriginal and Torres Strait Islander Peoples achieve food security?

Spatial Distribution of the Yam Daisy

Once you have completed your analysis you should present this as a paragraph using the following structure:

Pattern	What are you identifying? What pattern can you see? Where is it located?
Quantification	How can you use a number to describe the pattern? Why might the yam daisy be distributed in the pattern you identified earlier?
Exception	What have you observed that doesn't fit your pattern?

Lesson
BFS3

BIOMES AND FOOD SECURITY

How have Aboriginal and Torres Strait Islander Peoples changed biomes to produce food?

LEARNING INTENTIONS

- For students to analyse the impact that firestick farming has on the land
- For students to challenge Western assumptions about fire

KEY INQUIRY QUESTIONS

- What is **firestick farming**?
- What are the consequences of firestick farming on the land?
- How have people changed **biomes**?
- Should firestick farming be adopted as a method of managing the landscapes of rural Australia?

KEY VOCABULARY

firestick farming, terrestrial biomes, cultivated, controlled burns

TIME REQUIRED

45 minutes

HANDOUTS

- BFS 3.1 *Dark Emu* Synopsis – Fire; one per student
- BFS 3.2 Anticipation Guide; one per student
- BFS 3.3 Visual Source Analysis; one per student
- BFS 3.4 How Have Aboriginal and Torres Strait Islander peoples used fire as a tool?; one per student

TEACHER INSTRUCTIONS

PRIOR KNOWLEDGE

It is expected that students have learnt about:

1. The characteristics of major **terrestrial biomes** across Earth.
2. The range of biomes in Australia.

STARTER

1. Distribute handout BFS 3.2 'Anticipation Guide' to students to complete individually. They should respond to each statement, indicating whether they agree and write down the justification for their thoughts. You may wish to explain that these statements will preview the content of the day's lesson.
2. Discuss student answers as a class.

MAIN ACTIVITY

1. Distribute handout BFS 3.3 'Visual Source Analysis'. Ask students to use the visible thinking strategy of 'See Think Wonder' as prompted by the handout. You may have students come up to the board to collate responses or share with a friend.
2. Distribute handout BFS 3.1 Dark Emu Synopsis and handout BFS 3.4 'How Have Aboriginal and Torres Strait Islander peoples used fire as a tool?'. Ask students to complete the reading from *Dark Emu* and then the question sheet. Tell students to discuss and infer the disadvantages of using firestick farming.

PLENARY

1. Ask students to return to their Anticipation Guide and reflect on their initial answers. Ask which, if any, responses have changed. You may also ask them to check if they can answer all their 'wonders' as written in their visual source analysis.

DIFFERENTIATION

For less-able students:

- Ask students to define bolded words before reading the synopsis.
- Instruct students to work with a partner to complete the advantages and disadvantages of fire-stick farming (handout BFS 3.4, question 4). Assign one side to each partner then swap answers to complete the question.

For more-able students:

- Extend understanding by further discussing the concept of farming by distributing the article: http://www.theguardian.com.au/story/936405/the-first-farmers/.
- Extend understanding by researching the question, did firestick farming contribute to the extinction of megafauna?
- Analyse the use of firestick farming as a land management tool using SHEEPT factors (social, historical, environmental, economic, political, technological).

SUGGESTED ADAPTATIONS

To support kinaesthetic learners, the Anticipation Guide can be conducted as a whole class activity. Label each corner of the room as SA, A, D and SD and ask students to move to the corner that represents their response. Then ask one representative from each corner to explain their thinking.

Dark Emu Synopsis

Handout

BFS 3.1

How have Aboriginal and Torres Strait Islander Peoples changed biomes to produce food?

Fire

The use of fire has always played a central role in Australia's culture. Whilst fire is often viewed in Western society as a threat or danger, Aboriginal Australians hold a very different perspective. Some evidence suggests that Aboriginal Australians began using fire as early as 120,000 years ago, and researchers question whether its use contributed to the extinction of Australia's **megafauna**.

Fire is a tool which, when used responsibly, aids in the creation of a landscape that sustains life. One important way that Aboriginal Australians use fire is a practice called **firestick farming**. This involves planned and **controlled burns** of lower intensity in order to manage the **flora** and **fauna** within a **biome**. This approach to fire works on five principles:

1. The majority of lands were rotated through in patches or a **mosaic pattern** to allow plants and animals to survive in those not being burned
2. The timing of the fires was adjusted throughout the year, according to the type of country to be burned and the condition that it was already in
3. The **weather** conditions were strictly considered
4. Neighbouring **clans** communicated, advising each other of any fire activity
5. The burns were not to occur during the growing season of any plants.

Due to this principle of rotation, the land was **cultivated** into a pattern much like a mosaic, with sections of both **cleated land** and forest.

Firestick farming provides a method for regulating and managing the natural environment in order to maximise food resource. Better soils, produced after a burn, were used for food production while the inferior soils were left for forest. The preparation of soil is considered a signifier of **agriculture**.

It's important to recognise that this practice has had a significant impact on Australia's vegetation. Most obviously, Australia's **grasslands** increased. This became a way to control where animals would congregate to improve hunting and protect deliberate plantings from hungry animals. In turn, it marks a shift away from hunting big game and toward a reliance on cultivating grains and **tubers,** like the yam daisy.

A possibly more recognised advantage of firestick farming is the prevention of wildfires. When Aboriginal people were prevented from using this knowledge, underlying **vegetation** grew out of control and many native species suffered.

Source: Adapted from Pascoe, B 2018, *Dark Emu*: pp.161–176

Handout
BFS
3.2

How have Aboriginal and Torres Strait Islander Peoples changed biomes to produce food?

Anticipation Guide

Mark your opinion according to how strongly you feel, then provide an explanation of your thinking in the space provided.

SA: Strongly Agree **A**: Agree **D**: Disagree **SD**: Strongly Disagree

Statement	SA	A	D	SD	Explanation
Fire is dangerous.					
Fire should be considered a form of technology.					
Fires cause devastation to the landscape and should be avoided at all cost.					
Farming requires the planting of crops.					
When Europeans arrived, the landscape was dominated by trees and thick bush.					
The land as it was when Europeans arrived should be considered untouched and unmanaged.					
Australia's **biomes** remain constant over time.					

How have Aboriginal and Torres Strait Islander Peoples changed biomes to produce food?

Visual Source Analysis

Handout
BFS 3.3

Image: Watercolour Painting by Joseph Lycett, titled *Aborigines Using Fire to Hunt Kangaroos*, created c1817

See	Think	Wonder
What I can see in the image.	What I think this suggests.	Questions that I have about the image.

How have Aboriginal and Torres Strait Islander Peoples changed biomes to produce food?

How Was Fire Used as a Tool?

Handout **BFS 3.4**

After reading the synopsis for Bruce Pascoe's *Dark Emu*, answer the following:

1. In what ways can the Aboriginal and Torres Strait Islander peoples' use of fire be considered an agricultural p´actice?

2. If technology is defined as the application of scientific knowledge for practical purposes, do you think fire can be considered a form of technology?

3. In what ways has **firestick farming** changed Australia's **biomes**?

4. What are the advantages and disadvantages of firestick farming?

Advantages	Disadvantages

5. What aspects of contemporary life might present a challenge to the adoption of fire as a tool today?

Lesson

BFS4

BIOMES AND FOOD SECURITY

How can food production be managed to produce food sustainably in the future?

LEARNING INTENTIONS

- For students to understand the relationship between sustainable management of fishing and **food security**
- For students to examine the Brewarrina fish traps

KEY INQUIRY QUESTIONS

- What is **aquaculture**?
- How did the Brewarrina fish traps work?
- How might Indigenous fish traps become a model for the aquaculture industry?

KEY VOCABULARY

aquaculture, sustainability, overfishing

TIME REQUIRED

1 hour

HANDOUTS

- BFS 4.1 *Dark Emu* Synopsis – Aquaculture; one per student
- BFS 4.2 Brewarrina Fish Traps; one per student

TEACHER INSTRUCTIONS

PRIOR KNOWLEDGE

It is expected that students have learnt about:

1. Key determiners of food security – access, availability, appropriate use and stability over time.

STARTER

1. Distribute the following article to students. Ask them to complete a 'SIT' response – something Surprising, something Interesting and something Troubling about the article. Discuss as a class, highlighting the link between **overfishing** and **food insecurity**, threatening biodiversity in fresh waters. http://www.wildsingapore.com/news/20051112/051201-5.htm.

MAIN ACTIVITY

1. Introduce the day's case study by watching the story of the Brewarrina fish traps told by Aunty June Barker: a significant local elder https://youtu.be/sq0fDD8nPuU.
2. Distribute handout BFS 4.1 *Dark Emu* Synopsis – 'Aquaculture' and BFS 4.2 'Brewarrina Fish Traps' to students about Brewarrina.
3. Ask students to work with a partner to complete a reciprocal reading of the handouts as follows:
   a. In their pairs, students nominate partner A and partner B.
   b. Partner A begins by reading the first paragraph.
   c. Partner B then verbally summarises the information.
   d. Both partners write down 1–2 sentences as notes.
   e. This continues through each paragraph as students swap roles to share the reading.

PLENARY

1. Write the following five statements on the whiteboard:
   a. The **aquaculture** industry should incorporate ATSI approaches to fishing.
   b. **Overfishing** in lakes and rivers is overlooked.
   c. The model of fishing used at Brewarrina could be adopted elsewhere.
   d. The Brewarrina fish traps are an example of sustainable fishing.
   e. Sustainable management of fishing is a solution to **food security**.
2. Ask students to select three of the statements that they feel best illustrate what they learned in the lesson then justify their choices. You may collect this as a formative assessment.

DIFFERENTIATION

For less-able students:

- Students can watch this video on overfishing rather than read the starter article. Teachers will need to explain that overfishing happens in both oceans and rivers. https://www.youtube.com/watch?v=G8GRhkpOAgo
- Reduce the amount of reading by only giving the *Dark Emu* Synopsis.
- Create a graphic organiser for the reciprocal reading which includes a name or label for each paragraph and a space for the summary.

For more-able students:

- Read the entire starter article on overfishing.

SUGGESTED ADAPTATIONS

- It is highly recommended that for this lesson you flip the classroom and ask students to complete the starter activity for homework. This will reduce the amount of reading required during the class.
- Have students complete the plenary using 'flipgrid' online. They can record their justifications and upload it to the class page to view each other's responses. This is a great way to foster student voice.

How can food production be managed to produce food sustainably in the future?

Aquaculture

Handout **BFS 4.1**

Aboriginal Australians developed complex **aquaculture** techniques and expertise over centuries and these were immediately obvious to European colonists. In various parts of Victoria and New South Wales, Aboriginal Australians used rocks, clay and other natural materials to divert the flow of river water and to lead fish towards their nets. On the Murray River, a series of **dykes**, over a metre tall, were constructed. These acted as dams, which slowed the disappearance of water during summer and left shallow pools for fish to breed in. In some coastal areas, Aboriginal Australians even worked in partnership with killer whales and dolphins to drive fish toward the shore, where they could be easily caught and shared.

Of the established aquaculture structures early colonists observed, the massive fish traps at Brewarrina on the Darling River in New South Wales were some of the oldest and most successful. The traps are thousands of years old and are made up of large volcanic rocks carefully arranged in the river to guide and trap the fish. The traps have lasted as long as they have because they were constructed with incredible engineering skill – the stones are locked to the bed of the river so they don't wash away in floods.

But aquaculture is not only about catching fish; it also requires that there are enough fish breeding each year that there will be a reliable source of food for everyone. The Brewarrina fish traps were designed to allow breeding fish to pass upstream. Particular families managed particular ponds, but they each had a responsibility to ensure that other fisheries upstream, and downstream, had enough fish and that the entire system was **sustainable**.

Although the Brewarrina fish traps are heritage listed, many Aboriginal aquaculture systems were destroyed by European colonists in the first days of their arrival. Near Port Fairy in western Victoria, a village of around 200 people was burnt and its fishery was destroyed. There are many early accounts from colonists that describe the aquaculture structures and techniques they observed being used by Aboriginal Australians. But after 1880 there are very few texts that mention the existence of **fisheries** or other more or less complex processes of food production.

Source: Adapted from Pascoe 2018, *Dark Emu* pp.68–87

Handout

BFS 4.2

How can food production be managed to produce food sustainably in the future?

Brewarrina Fish Traps

The traditional Aboriginal fish traps at Brewarrina, also known as Baiame's Ngunnhu, on the Barwon River in north-west NSW are estimated to be 40,000 years old, making them some of the oldest human-made structures on earth. They are approximately half a kilometre long and the largest in Australia. They have been listed on the Australian National Heritage List since 2005. The fish traps are an inventive and advanced system of rocks that herd fish through sections of the river, allowing them to be caught during high and low rivers. This practice was sustainable as it allowed smaller fish through, ensuring future spawning opportunities.

The Brewarrina fish traps hold incredible traditional, spiritual and cultural significance to the Aboriginal people, as well as forming an important part of their subsistence. It was a part of their travel and trade routes, and it is a meeting place for over 20 nations including the Ngemba, who are the custodians of the fishery.

The area has undergone significant changes since the inhabitation by Europeans in the early nineteenth century. The clearing of land, water diversion for crops, introduction of weeds, rubbish and construction of a weir have resulted in lower water levels which in turn has impacted on the number of fish and overall health of the **ecosystem**.

Source: Text adapted from http://www.riverspace.com.au/item/baiames-ngunnhu-brewarrina-fish-traps/ and https://www.environment.nsw.gov.au/heritageapp/ViewHeritageItemDetails.aspx?ID=5051305.]

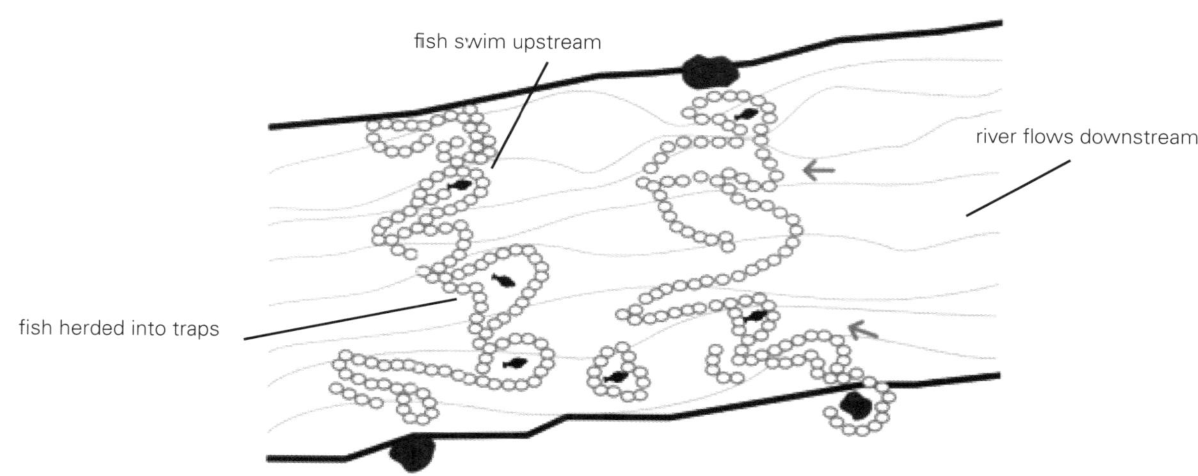

Lesson
BFS5

BIOMES AND FOOD SECURITY

What role could Indigenous strategies play in ensuring food security across Australia?

LEARNING INTENTIONS

- For students to reflect on increasing population as a challenge to **food security**
- For students to explore the role of Aboriginal and Torres Strait Islander strategies in food production

KEY INQUIRY QUESTIONS

- How has Australia's population changed over time?
- What role could ATSI strategies play in ensuring food security across Australia?

KEY VOCABULARY

sustainable practice

TIME REQUIRED

1 hour

MATERIALS

- Post-it™ notes; one per student

HANDOUTS

- BFS 5.1 *Dark Emu* Synopsis – Sustainability; one per student
- BFS 5.2 Australian Population Statistics; one per student

TEACHER INSTRUCTIONS

PRIOR KNOWLEDGE

It is expected that students have learnt about:

1. Key determiners of **food security** – access, availability, appropriate use and stability over time.
2. The link between population growth and food security.

STARTER

1. Distribute Post-it™ notes to students and ask them to write down their understanding of the term sustainable.
2. Watch the video introducing ATSI perspectives on **sustainability** http://education.abc.net.au/home#!/media/525907/.
3. Ask students how this compares to their understanding.

MAIN ACTIVITY

1. Distribute handout BFS 5.2 'Australian population statistics'. Ask students to create a line graph of Australia's population based on the data then answer the questions in the handout. See page 50 for assistance using the method.
2. Distribute handout BFS 5.1 *Dark Emu* Synopsis – Sustainability. You may wish to read this as a class. If you have completed other lessons from this resource, you can draw on the new knowledge to create links.
3. Pose the following essential question to the class:
   a. Given the population has increased so significantly, what role, if any, could Indigenous strategies play in ensuring food security across Australia?

4. Conduct a line debate to discuss responses:
   a. Arrange the students in two lines facing each other. Be sure to place vocal students on different sides.
   b. Students make statements supporting their position with one person speaking at a time.
   c. Any time a valid point is made, they may select a student from the opposing line to join their side.
   d. The team with the most students at the end wins.

PLENARY

1. Ask students to write a short paragraph responding to the essential question explaining their reasons.

DIFFERENTIATION

For less-able students:

- Provide students with a template for the graph with the axes drawn up and labelled.

For more-able students:

- Have students research Indigenous strategies that may be a solution to **food insecurity**.

Dark Emu Synopsis

What role could Indigenous strategies play in ensuring food security across Australia?

Sustainability

Handout **BFS 5.1**

Indigenous people have always practised a range of **management strategies** to maintain balance in Australia's **ecosystem**. This has included soil management, fishing with traps in rivers and animal farming.

Soil management for agricultural processes has been documented by a number of colonists. One method for ensuring good quality soil involved **controlled burns** to maintain productive Aboriginal land. This involved a routine in which sections of land were burnt periodically to promote growth in what is considered a planned program of **cropping**. While these burns increased carbon in the soil, they also prevented understory species from overwhelming the land.

Aboriginal fishing systems were not only about catching food but ensuring that there were enough fish breeding each year to provide a reliable source of food for everyone. The Brewarrina fish traps were designed to allow breeding fish to pass upstream. Particular families managed particular ponds, but they each had a responsibility to ensure that other fisheries upstream, and downstream, had enough fish and that the entire system was sustainable.

Another sustainable food practice was that of harvesting animals. **Kangaroo harvesting** is particularly notable in this regard. Modern researchers speculate that the methods used did not harm the population of the species as only adult males were targeted. This allowed for those not captured to continue to breed. In the case of ducks and other fowl, nets were used to catch them but were strung up only temporarily so as not to interrupt natural migration patterns.

But these **sustainable practices** were disrupted when Australia was colonised by the British. Many people can recognise the displacement of Aboriginal peoples as a direct impact of **colonisation**. Often, the impact on the land is overlooked. The arrival of these newcomers saw the rapid worsening of the land's natural environment.

Source: Adapted from Pascoe 2018, *Dark Emu*, pp.10–1, 51–2, 74–5, 164–71.

What role could Indigenous strategies play in ensuring food security across Australia?

Handout
BFS 5.2

Australian Population Statistics

Based on the data on the chart below, create a line graph plotting Australia's population since 1980. Your x-axis should have the years, and y-axis, the population. It is recommended you start at 12 million and go to 25 million. Ensure you use a consistent scale (i.e. 0.5cm represents 1 million years or 1cm represents 1 million years). Ensure your graph has SALTS (scale, axis (labelled), legend, title and source).

Year	Population	Year	Population
1980	14 726 700	2001	19 603 502
1983	15 451 900	2004	20 229 800
1986	16 028 400	2007	21 180 600
1989	16 957 100	2010	22 477 400
1992	17 568 700	2013	23 319 400
1995	18 173 600	2016	24 385 600
1998	18 871 800	2018	25 000 000

Source: Australian Bureau of Statistics 2018

Once you have constructed the graph, answer these questions in your workbooks:

1. Use PQE (pattern, quantification, exception) to explain the overall trend of the graph.
2. How much did Australia's population grow by between 1980 and 2016?
3. Between which three years do you notice the greatest growth?
4. Between which three years do you notice the slowest growth?
5. Predict Australia's population in 2025.

Environmental Change and Management

YEAR 10 | STAGE 5

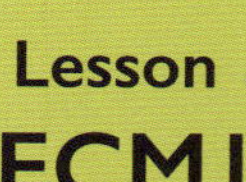

Lesson ECM1

ENVIRONMENTAL CHANGE AND MANAGEMENT

How have Australian environments been changed?

LEARNING INTENTIONS

- For students to understand land management strategies used by Aboriginal and Torres Strait Islanders
- For students to identify how Australian environments have changed over time

KEY INQUIRY QUESTIONS

- What was the Australian environment like prior to **colonisation**?
- How do Aboriginal and Torres Strait Islanders manage the land?
- How has the Australian environment changed since colonisation?

KEY VOCABULARY

sustainability, saltwater intrusion, rom

TIME REQUIRED

90 minutes

MATERIALS

- Internet access or relevant printouts from Arafura Swamp Rangers Healthy Country Plan; students receive one set
- Labels A, B, C & D for corners of the room
- Post-it™ notes; three per student

HANDOUT

- ECM1 *Dark Emu* Synopsis – Australian Environments; one per student

TEACHER INSTRUCTIONS

PRIOR KNOWLEDGE

It is expected that students have learnt about:

1. An overview of salinity, desertification and erosion causing land degradation.

STARTER

Student quiz on land degradation:

1. Label corners of the room A, B, C and D.
2. Read out each question and ask students to move to the corner they think is labelled with the correct answer.
3. Distribute handout ECM 1 *Dark Emu* synopsis, 'Australian Environments' for students to read.
4. Using the information from the *Dark Emu* synopsis and their prior knowledge, have students answer these questions in their workbooks:

- What was the Australian environment like prior to colonisation?
- How do/have Aboriginal and Torres Strait Islanders manage/d the land?
- Has this changed over time?
- How has the environment changed since colonisation?

MAIN ACTIVITY

1. Read page 42 of the management of Arafura case study, as a class. https://www.bushheritage.org.au/getattachment/places-we-protect/northern-territory/arafura/ASRAC-HCP-2017.pdf?lang=en-AU.
2. Put students into five groups. Each group is given a few topics on 'threats to our country and vision'

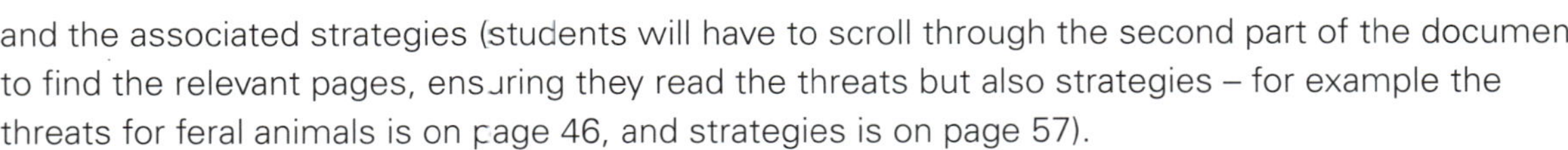

and the associated strategies (students will have to scroll through the second part of the document to find the relevant pages, ensuring they read the threats but also strategies – for example the threats for feral animals is on page 46, and strategies is on page 57).

GROUPS

1. Empty Country, Loss of Respect for **Rom** and Elders and Wrong People on Country
2. Commercial Fishing and Lack of Jobs on Country
3. Feral Animals and Weeds
4. **Saltwater Intrusion** (and **Climate** Change) and Bad Fire
5. Balanda Rules Always Changing and Mining

3. In their groups, students should read both the threats and strategies on their topics and answer these questions:
   - What are the threats?
   - How does it impact the Aboriginal people in the Arafura Swamp area?
   - What outcome are they hoping for?
   - What strategies are being implemented?
4. Using this information, student groups should then present it in one of two ways:
   - As an infographic — students should ensure all key points are included as well as appropriate visuals.
   - As a radio/TV interview — students should choose and assign appropriate roles (such as government minister, National Parks ranger, etc.) in their groups and ensure all key points are covered. (This could be uploaded to Flipgrid as a video and students could view and comment on each other's.)
5. Students then share their information with the class.

CONCLUSION

1. Have students go back to their initial questions and add any information to them (particularly the management questions).
2. Ticket out the door:
   Provide students with three Post-it™ notes each. Have them write down:
   - Three things they learnt
   - Two questions they have
   - One final reflection

DIFFERENTIATION

For less-able students:

- Students should be assigned to group 2 (less reading) or 3 (more straightforward content).
- Students write one point for each 'ticket out the door.'

For more-able students:

- At the end of their investigation, have students answer the question: Why are some management strategies more effective than others?
- Have students examine all threats and compare the effectiveness of their strategies. Could these strategies be applied to other locations?

SUGGESTED ADAPTATIONS

- Put the quiz questions on a slide to support visual learners. You could also create a quick Kahoot on the topic.

Dark Emu Synopsis

How have Australian environments been changed?

Australian Environments

Handout **ECM 1**

The eviction of Aboriginal people from their land was succeeded by the rapid deterioration of the soil. Farmers noticed a startling decline in the productivity of the soil in a short time frame, as sheep and cattle ate the native crops and compacted the soil. Pascoe quoted farmer and historian Eric Rolls: *In Australia thousands of years of grass and soil changed in a few years. The spongy soil grew hard, the run-off accelerated and different grasses dominated.* (quoted in Pascoe, 2018, pp. 10–1)

The colonists did not know that the fertile soil was due to careful management by Aboriginal Australians, and cultural blindness ensured they would never blame themselves for the degradation. The management of the land was intentional, not accidental as we are sometimes led to believe. *Aboriginal people were not reacting to the state of nature but directly affecting its production.* (Pascoe, 2018, p. 63).

Evidence from colonists and settlers likens the Australian landscape to *the manicured parks of England* (Gammage, B 2011, p. 242 in Pascoe, 2018 p. 164); that is, moderately dotted with trees, free from undergrowth and maintained.

The use of fire to clear the landscape is well documented: *Aboriginal people used fire as a tool for increasing the productivity of their environment.* (Kohen, J 1993, p. 4 in Pascoe, 2018, p. 165). There is also evidence of **terracing** of yam gardens, of wells and **irrigation** trenches used to water crops.

Archeologist Rhys Jones best sums it up: *What do we want to conserve, the environment as it was in 1788, or do we yearn for an environment without man, as it might have been 30,000 or more years ago? If the former, then we must do what the Aborigines did and burn at regular intervals under controlled conditions.* (Jones, R 1969 in Pascoe, 2018, p. 166). This can be applied to most Aboriginal land management strategies — we should be learning from how the Aboriginal and Torres Strait Islanders managed the land, as they had done so very effectively for thousands of years.

Source: Adapted from Pascoe, B 2018, *Dark Emu*, pp.10–26, 46–50, 64–8.

STUDENT QUIZ ON LAND DEGRADATION

1. What percentage of Australia's farmland is currently degraded?
   A. 15%
   B. 50%
   C. 65%
   D. 90%

2. What are the two greatest causes of land degradation?
   A. Industry and mining
   B. Energy production and pollution
   C. Crop growing and wood collection
   D. Overgrazing and deforestation

3. Which of the following might result from overgrazing?
   A. Desertification
   B. Introduction of exotic species
   C. Alteration of plant communities
   D. All of the above

4. The main cause of erosion is:
   A. Overgrazing of hard-hooved animals causing soil compaction
   B. Too much rainfall caused by **climate** change
   C. Poor internal drainage
   D. Low organic matter

5. Which of the following is not an impact of land degradation?
   A. Habitat loss
   B. Water scarcity
   C. **Food insecurity**
   D. Loss of topsoil

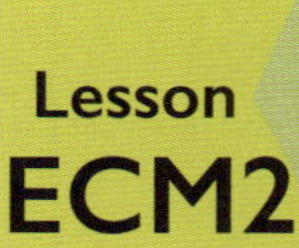

Lesson
ECM2

ENVIRONMENTAL CHANGE AND MANAGEMENT

Does the consumption of kangaroo meat have a future in Australia?

LEARNING INTENTIONS

- For students to have an understanding of the kangaroo industry and the different stakeholders involved
- For students to examine an issue from a range of perspectives

KEY INQUIRY QUESTION

- What is **kangaroo harvesting**?
- What are the benefits of eating kangaroo?
- What are the downsides of kangaroo harvesting?
- Is kangaroo farming a viable solution to land degradation caused by overgrazing?

KEY VOCABULARY

macropods, harvested, quota

TIME REQUIRED

40 min – 1 hour

MATERIALS

- Group labels (A4 paper with name printed)

HANDOUTS

- ECM 2.1 Dark Emu Synopsis – Kangaroo Harvesting
- ECM 2.2 – Overview of the Kangaroo Industry; one for each student
- ECM 2.3 – Group Information Cards; one or two per group
- ECM 2.4 – Scenario Cards; one per group

TEACHER INSTRUCTIONS

PRIOR KNOWLEDGE

It is expected that students have learnt about:

- Land degradation.
- The impact of hard-hooved animals on land in Australia.

SETTING UP

- Set up the room in a horse-shoe, with separate tables for each group.
- Place a group name label at the front of each group table.

STARTER

Distribute handout ECM 2.1 *Dark Emu* synopsis 'Kangaroo Harvesting'. Explain to students they will be participating in a role play on the kangaroo industry.

MAIN ACTIVITY

1. Introduction

- Distribute handout ECM 2.2 'Overview of the Kangaroo Industry and Task Instructions' and the relevant handout ECM 2.3 'Group Information Card' to each group.
- Ask students to read and discuss their information in their groups. Tell students to introduce their group to the class (who they are and what they believe). From now on, students should act in character for the rest of the activity.

2. Round 1

Present students handout ECM 2.4 with Scenario 1. Give them five minutes to freely discuss their response in their groups. Each group should present their views on the topic. Allow some free discussion following the presentations.

3. Round 2

Present students handout ECM 2.4 with Scenario 2. Allow them five minutes to discuss it in their groups, focusing on the key points:

- How do you feel about this?
- How does this affect you?
- What do you think needs to be done?
- Are there any other possible solutions to the problem?

Allow each group time to share their response, and also time for unstructured discussion.

4. Conclusion

Encourage the class to come to a consensus on the issue. You may even want to consider a vote.

5. Debrief

Ask students to bring a chair into the middle and sit in a circle inside the tables. Have them mix up and sit next to different students. Pose these questions and allow free discussion:

- How did it feel to be in your position?
- Did you change your mind about anything?
- What did you learn?

PLENARY

Ask students to write a 300–500 word reflection on the activity. Including the following:

- What role did you play and what was your group position?
- What are pros and cons of **kangaroo harvesting**?
- Your personal belief on the questions: Is kangaroo farming a viable solution to land degradation caused by overgrazing? And why?

DIFFERENTIATION

For less-able students:

- Ensure they are in a group with supportive students. Encourage them to join in the small group discussions.

For more-able students:

- When completing the reflection, students should conduct additional research into the kangaroo industry. Can they find any other stakeholders who should have been involved in the discussion?

SUGGESTED ADAPTATIONS

- If this type of activity is not appropriate for your class then you could do it as a jigsaw activity – have students in expert groups, each exploring a stakeholder's perspective, then break out into mixed groups – one 'stakeholder' in each new group. They could then have small group discussions.
- Provide students with a number of different stakeholder information and have them read it and examine the issue from a range of perspectives.
- Give students their group ahead of time and have them conduct further research into the stakeholder.

Dark Emu Synopsis

Does the consumption of kangaroo meat have a future in Australia?

Kangaroo Harvesting

Handout
ECM 2.1

Aboriginal peoples were noted, by colonists, to engage in **game drives** over 30 kilometres long. It was a collaborative effort, with a couple of thousand people from a number of tribes joining in the hunt together. They used large nets and brush fences to herd the animals to holding pens where they could either release them or slaughter them.

Experts speculate that kangaroo populations were not impacted by the hunting as adult males were targeted. A 2002 study by scientists discovered that **harvesting** 10,000 males over eight years actually saw a population increase of kangaroos.

Kangaroo meat has a low-fat content and is free from **chemical impurities**. They can tolerate Australia's harsh conditions and their soft hooves don't **degrade** the land like **hard-hooved** sheep and cattle.

Resource use is a current challenge to Australia. Our lands are being degraded by current farming methods. Our cities are struggling to meet our water demands.

We really need to change the way we think about how Aboriginal people managed the land and, not only that, learn from them. What if we considered a native species as a **sustainable** meat source? It makes sense to choose animals that are best adapted for our land, and make fewer demands on our water supply. Kangaroos and other **macropods** are perfect for this. Harvesting kangaroos and wallabies will not harm their population, it will protect it. Our current farming methods are having devastating impacts on the environment. Hard-hooved cattle and sheep cause extensive land degradation and erosion, yet kangaroos are adapted to our **climate** and geography and do little damage.

Gordon Grigg (in Pascoe 2018, pp. 63–4) argues that:

> *Graziers already run sheep on top of kangaroos (and other herbivores) and the grazing pressure is too high. If they make money from kangaroos, and if the kangaroos become accepted as an economically positive part of their mixed grazing system, they will at least have an option of maintaining economic viability with lower sheep numbers.*

Farmers are industrious and flexible; they have shown this time and time again, changing to suit consumers needs. One of the biggest roadblocks is consumers' disgust at eating native fauna. If we are able to alter our views and look objectively, then harvesting wild animals such as kangaroos and emus makes perfect sense.

Aboriginal people have extensive knowledge of the **sustainability** of the land and all that comes with it. Let's embrace that and change our current degrading ways.

Adapted from Pascoe, B 2018, Dark Emu, pp.51–3 & 163–217.

Does the consumption of kangaroo meat have a future in Australia?

Overview of the Kangaroo Industry

Handout
ECM
2.2

Introduction to the Kangaroo Industry

Key points:

- Kangaroo meat is not 'farmed' as such – but harvested from the wild
- Kangaroos are 'soft footed' animals and very suited to our **climate** and landscape
- Kangaroo meat is lean and healthy
- Kangaroos have a smaller carbon footprint
- Kangaroo meat is exported around the world

Four species of kangaroo are commonly harvested – red kangaroos, eastern and western grey kangaroos, and the common wallaroo. Harvesting occurs in four states – NSW, WA, QLD and SA, and is regulated within each state by the relevant government authority. Management plans for the harvest, however, must be approved by the federal government.

Kangaroo meat is very healthy – it has less than 2% fat, most of which is polyunsaturated. As it is harvested from the wild, it contains no added hormones, chemicals, or antibiotics. It is very high in iron and protein. It does, however, contain L-carnitine, a compound found in all red meat but which is highest in kangaroo. It is associated with the build-up of arterial plaque (which may lead to heart attacks, cardiovascular disease and strokes), if eaten in excess.

A maximum **quota** of 15–20% of the kangaroo population can be harvested in any year, but usually much less than that is taken. And population surveys are conducted regularly to keep an eye on kangaroo numbers. There is a policy that only male kangaroos are harvested; this is to ensure the **sustainability** of the kangaroo population.

Kangaroos damage crops and equipment such as fences, and farmers consider them a 'pest'. For many years farmers killed kangaroos themselves, so having this cull regulated and turned into profit is a win-win situation – for both farmers and the environment. Currently the kangaroo industry creates 4000 jobs (2000 direct and 2000 indirect), and generates $200 million for the Australian economy.

Sources: https://www.choice.com.au/food-and-drink/meat-fish-and-eggs/meat/articles/kangaroo-meat
http://www.kangarooindustry.com/

Task

You will be participating in a forum on the future of the kangaroo industry. You will represent one group (or stakeholder) and need to act in character for this activity.

In your group, read the information provided. Discuss it and briefly summarise it – who you are and what you believe. You will need to introduce yourselves soon.

Does the consumption of kangaroo meat have a future in Australia?

Group Information Cards

Handout **ECM 2.3** (1 of 3)

ANIMAL RIGHTS ACTIVISTS

You are an animal rights group that is concerned for the welfare of all animals. In particular your concern about the kangaroo industry is the lack of regulation. You think slaughtering innocent animals is awful, and are vegan.

Even though it is mandated that kangaroos are killed by a single shot to the head, it is estimated that 100,000 are not killed in this way. You are concerned about the long and painful deaths these animals face. There are no statistics for any animals that are shot and injured but escape. You don't think the industry is well regulated at all.

Joeys are a concern too. If a mother is killed and has a joey then it is considered kinder to kill the joey than to leave it to starve.

CONSUMER

You think kangaroo meat is healthy and sustainable, but are concerned about the treatment of kangaroos. You are a little confused at all the conflicting information out there. Kangaroos have less diseases than most other meats (such as beef and lamb), and they do not contain hormones or chemicals. They are naturally 'organic'.

You like the fact that kangaroos are better for the environment. Cows and sheep belch out large amounts of methane, a greenhouse gas 20 times more potent than carbon dioxide. Kangaroos, on the other hand, produce very little of it. So switching to kangaroo can help ease your carbon footprint.

Kangaroos also have less impact on the land compared to cattle and sheep, according to Dr Rosie Cooney from the University of NSW 'Kangaroos have a much lower environmental impact in terms of water used,' she says. 'Cattle and sheep also have hard hooves, which causes land degradation and increases soil erosion.'

There are many reasons to choose kangaroo as a red meat. Compared to sheep and cattle, kangaroos' impact on the environment is minimal. Though it takes about one and a half kangaroos to provide as much usable meat for human consumption as a sheep (around 12kg from a kangaroo, and around 18kg from a sheep), kangaroos need less feed and water.

Source: https://www.choice.com.au/food-and-drink/meat-fish-and-eggs/meat/articles/kangaroo-meat

KANGAROO INDUSTRY

The kangaroo industry is the organisation that oversees and promotes **kangaroo harvesting** for meat and products. You believe that kangaroo meat is healthy, sustainable and that culling kangaroos is important for environmental balance. Kangaroo meat is now regularly exported to over 40 countries worldwide, and is worth an estimated $150 million annually to the Australian economy.

The industry is arguably the most sustainable and has one of the best practices in the world. The kangaroos live naturally, grazing on **pasture** and foliage of the Australian bush. You take animal welfare very seriously. You have worked closely with the various government departments to help regulate the industry. You are concerned what would happen to the kangaroo population if there was no harvesting – they could spiral out of control and many animals would die of starvation during times of drought.

Kangaroos have always been hunted – by people and dingoes. European **colonisation** has greatly changed what was a happy cohabitation between Aboriginals and animals for thousands of years. The commercial **harvest** is a replacement of Aboriginal hunting and dingo predation; it helps maintain a natural balance.

Source: http://www.kangarooindustry.com/

Does the consumption of kangaroo meat have a future in Australia?

Group Information Cards

ACADEMIC GROUP

A THINK TANK FOR KANGAROO HARVESTING

You are an organisation based out of a university, which is partly funded by an animal protection group. You have researched the subject of kangaroo culling and your report says you do not support the cull of kangaroos. You think that a lot of the information supporting the cull of kangaroos is incorrect, and you also think the industry in inhumane.

You think that the argument that kangaroos steal cattle food is incorrect, and only occurs during a drought. You don't think that farmers would choose to farm kangaroos insead of livestock because there are not enough 'roos to fill the current demand for meat in Australia, let alone an international market.

Your report also found significant reductions in greenhouse gases from livestock would only occur if kangaroo meat consumption replaced beef and lamb demand.

You think the government should also ban the killing of female kangaroos, which often have joeys in their pouches or with them.

Source: http://thinkkangaroos.uts.edu.au/

BRUCE PASCOE

ABORIGINAL WRITER AND HISTORIAN, OF BUNURONG/TASMANIAN HERITAGE

Harvesting kangaroos and wallabies will not endanger the population of **macropods** but instead guarantee their protection. We just have to accept the fact that if we are going to source protein in the form of animal flesh it would make sense to use the animals best adapted to our soils and **climate**, those which do least damage to our soil and make least demands on our dwindling water supplies.

Animal rights and welfare groups quite rightly monitor the production methods of farms and the treatment of domestic animals, but the national abhorrence for the consumption of native fauna is threatening our soils and water supplies. Utilising these animals does not means they will never again be 'seen in the wild'. Rather, it guarantees that they will, whereas our current methods are seeing mass extinctions of animals adapted to an environment previously managed and shapes by Aboriginal Australia.

We need to be consulted on this. We have been here forever, since the Dreaming, and have managed the land very effectively until the arrival of white man.

Source: Pascoe, B 2014, *Dark Emu*: Black Seeds: agriculture or accident?, pp.148

Does the consumption of kangaroo meat have a future in Australia?

Group Information Cards

Handout **ECM 2.3**

CATTLE FARMERS

You are cattle farmers on a large station. You see kangaroos as pests. They eat food meant for your stock and, without natural predators like dingoes keeping their numbers down, are a real problem. They are particularly problematic during a drought, when times are tough enough already. You think the killing of kangaroos is vital to your livelihood.

It is illegal to shoot kangaroos without a licence, and there are strict limits on the number of permits issued. Farmers and professional hunters can apply to the National Parks office for a permit. You would like three times the current number of kangaroos harvested; they are in plague proportions and something needs to be done to protect your farm and business. You would like to see changes to the current licensing laws.

You think that if you were able to cull more kangaroos, this would supplement your income greatly. You think the government needs to look beyond traditional means of protein sources. If you could make more money from kangaroos it would give you more reason to value the native environment, and reduce your sheep and cattle population.

Source: http://www.abc.net.au/news/rural/2017-09-29/kangaroo-management-fails-farmers-in-record-roo-numbers/8993148

DEPARTMENT OF ENVIRONMENT AND ENERGY

You are the government department responsible for the management of kangaroo culling. You work in conjunction with the state departments in NSW, WA, QLD and SA to oversee the industry, including permits and treatment of animals.

'It is [the department's] view that kangaroos do cause damage and economic loss to the farming community, the extent of which does vary across the landscape.' The commercial kangaroo **harvest** industry in Australia is one of the world's best practice wild harvest operations, with management goals based firmly on principles of **sustainability**.

You have put strict rules in place which govern how kangaroos should be harvested, and **quotas** which dictate how many can be taken. You regularly monitor the population of kangaroos and update the quotas accordingly. You consider annual harvest levels in the order of 15 percent of the populations for grey kangaroos and wallaroos, and 20 percent for red kangaroos, are sustainable. Quotas recognise the maximum number that can be taken, and generally less than 65% of the total quota is actually harvested.

https://www.smh.com.au/environment/conservation/food-for-thought-as-roo-culling-reasons-come-under-fire-20101128-18cfz.html

Does the consumption of kangaroo meat have a future in Australia?

Scenario Cards

Scenario 1

The government is looking to increase **quotas** on kangaroos by 10%. Do you support this? Why/why not?

Scenario 2

Most of Australia's agricultural areas have been destroyed by erosion and desertification. The price of beef and lamb has risen by 10 times as there are very few viable farms. Consumers are frustrated and looking elsewhere. Is kangaroo meat the future of the Australian meat industry? What should be done?

Points to discuss in your group:

- How do you feel about this?
- How does this affect you?
- What do you think needs to be done?
- Are there any other possible solutions to the problem?

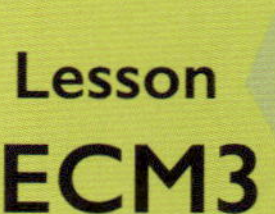

Lesson ECM3

ENVIRONMENTAL CHANGE AND MANAGEMENT

Is revegetation with native species a viable solution to land degradation?

LEARNING INTENTIONS

- For students to understand **revegetation**
- For students to examine satellite images and identify changes over time

KEY INQUIRY QUESTIONS

- What is revegetation and what does it involve?
- What are the benefits of revegetation?
- Why is revegetation a sustainable management approach?

KEY VOCABULARY

revegetation, sustainability

TIME REQUIRED

45 minutes

HANDOUTS

- ECM 3.1 *Dark Emu* Synopsis – Revegetation
- ECM 3.2 Satellite Images
- ECM 3.3 Revegetation Introduction
- ECM 3.4 Revegetation Case Study
- ECM 3.5 Frayer Graphic Organiser

TEACHER INSTRUCTIONS

PRIOR KNOWLEDGE

It is expected that students have learnt about:

1. Land degradation caused by historical issues such as introduction of non-indigenous species and destruction of native vegetation.

STARTER

1. Distribute handout ECM 3.2 'Satellite Images' to student pairs. Instruct students to examine the satellite images and answer the following questions:
   - What change has occurred between 2006 and 2013?
   - What human activities have taken place between 2006 and 2013?
   - What impact do you think this would have on the **sustainability** of the area?

MAIN ACTIVITIES

1. Distribute handout ECM 3.1 *Dark Emu* Synopsis – Revegetation.
2. Ask students to read handout ECM 3.3 'Revegetation Introduction' and handout ECM 3.4 'Revegetation Case Study' to provide them with background information to revegetation.
3. Students should use the information provided to create a poster or infographic on the topic 'revegetation is a sustainable management approach'.

PLENARY

1. Distribute handout ECM 3.5 – 'Frayer Graphic Organiser' and have students use it to complete notes on revegetation. Students should write 'revegetation' in the central circle.

Students follow the prompts to note down a definition, key characteristics and examples. Key characteristics refers to the main features of revegetation. Examples could include Battery Creek, Yan Yan Gurt Creek and Mullocn Creek (https://themullooninstitute.org/projects/), but students could also research their own. Non-examples mean things that aren't an example of revegetation. For example, using non-natives, afforestation or 'natural revegetation' (allowing nature to take its course).

2. Lastly, have students give revegetation a ranking out of 10 for how effective they think it would be as a tool to counteract land degradation.

DIFFERENTIATION

For less-able students:

- Have students define the key words in the revegetation handout prior to reading.
- Pre-fill an example and a non-example for the student in the graphic organiser.
- Some of the lessons here might be appropriate for your students: http://seed.vic.gov.au/Resources/seed/217_biodiversity%20unit%201%20planting%20an%20idea.pdf or, explore the 'Unit 1: Planting an idea' resource available here: http://seed.vic.gov.au/Resources/Curriculum/tpk/20/lvl/2.

For more-able students:

- Have students investigate and compare revegetation programs in other countries.
- Have students investigate the Battery Creek revegetation project as seen in the satellite images. https://greenfleet.com.au/Our-forests/Planting-Sites/Battery-Creek. Was it an effective project? What evidence is there to support this?

SUGGESTED ADAPTATIONS

- Is there somewhere in your local area that needs revegetation? Contact your local council or the Department of **Sustainability** for further information. Your local nursery should have information about and tubestock or seeds of species native to your area.
- The activities on the SEED (School Environment Education Directory north east) website are aimed at younger students, but Activity 4 – the revegetation project, could easily be adapted for older students: http://seed.vic.gov.au/Resources/seed/217_biodiversity%20unit%201%20planting%20an%20idea.pdf.

Dark Emu Synopsis

Handout **ECM 3.1**

Is revegetation with native species a viable solution to land degradation?

Revegetation

Fragility of the soil recorded within a few years of **colonisation** and the impacts of **hard-hooved** animals such as goats, sheep and horses were evident. *'Once the soil hardened, rains ran off the compacted surfaces and rivers flooded higher than the Aboriginals had ever seen them. This created new management problems for the soils of this district and others.'* (Pascoe, 2018, p. 23). This early record of erosion really highlights the impact the colonists had on the land in such a short period of time.

Colonist Isaac Batey made remarkable records of what he saw, including this in 1864:

> *Where once abundant they have become quite extinct for the district where the writer was raised in this 1909 might be searched without discovering a solitary example ... Elsewhere it has been intimated that our domestic animals had eaten them out, yet there was another factor of destruction in the soil becoming hardened with the continuous tramping of sheep cattle or horses. In proof of that, Mr. Edward Page said "When we first same here I started a vegetable garden, the soil dug like ashes." It has to be added it was a spot free of timber or scrub of any description, the soil a reddish loam of great depth.*
>
> (Batey, Quoted In Frankel, D 1982, 'An Account of Aboriginal Use of the Yam Daisy', *The Artefact*, Vol 7 (1–2), P. 44, Quoted In Pascoe, 2018, P. 21–2)

This highlights the destruction of the landscape and disappearance of the yam daisy, just a few years after colonists arrived in the Melbourne area.

Aboriginals were precise with the soils they used and how they managed them:

> *Aboriginals left forest on the poor quality lands and used fire to clear the best soils to create pastures and croplands.*
>
> (Pascoe, 2018 p. 4).

So much can be learnt from Aboriginal management of the soil, and yet colonists ignored the methods they described. We can only assume it was a combination of ignorance and cultural blindness, because it is clear that the land was well managed prior to colonists, and degraded in such a short period of time after their arrival.

It is important to highlight the difference between introduced and native plant species:

> *The great advantage of Aboriginal crops is that they have been developed through seed selection, direct planting and weeding for the harsh conditions of Australia. Many of the grains grow on sand and require a minimum of irrigation.*
>
> (Pascoe, 2018 p. 67)

Source: Adapted from Pascoe, B 2018, *Dark Emu*, pp. 21–7 & 67

Is revegetation with native species a viable solution to land degradation?

Satellite Images

Handout ECM 3.2

To view the maps go to:

https://greenfleet.com.au/Blog/ArtMID/3250/ArticleID/18/Stunning-before-and-after-pictures-of-Battery-Creek-one-of-our-revegetation-projects-in-South-Gippland-Vic

Is revegetation with native species a viable solution to land degradation?

Revegetation Introduction

Handout **ECM 3.3**

When colonists arrived, native vegetation was wiped out by grazing livestock and removed so crops could be planted. Native Australian plants are suited to our **climate** and soil. They are deep rooted and help keep the water table low, avoiding salinity issues.

Revegetation involves the planting of native species on land that has been degraded through human processes such as salinity, desertification and erosion. On private land in north-east Victoria, only 17 per cent of the original native vegetation remains.

Effective revegetation has many benefits:

- Reduces soil and water loss
- Improves soil fertility
- Provides a habitat for native species
- Improves water quality
- Controls salinity
- Stabilises soil
- Acts as sink for greenhouse gases
- Provides shelter for livestock and crops
- Assists with crop pollination
- Improves agricultural outcomes

To ensure revegetation is successful, attempts should be made to find out what the natural vegetation was like prior to degradation. This can be achieved by profiling similar healthy vegetation communities. Ideally revegetation involves the removal of weeds, preparing the soil, pest management which may include fencing, and planting a wide range of appropriate native plant species.

Revegetation can take place on any degraded land – public or private. Farmers often find it useful to revegetate parts of their land as it improves the overall quality of their soil and can assist with crop pollination and reduces soil erosion.

It is more desirable to prevent degradation than engage in revegetation; however, once land is degraded it is fortunate there are solutions.

In recent years the Australian Government has encouraged revegetation of degraded areas through the funding of various projects.

Is revegetation with native species a viable solution to land degradation?

Revegetation Case Study

Handout ECM 3.4

The Yan Yan Gurt Creek story

I wanted to reflect on my involvement as a farmer in a catchment revegetation project over 20 years. It's the Yan Yan Gurt Creek catchment in the south of Victoria. The motivation for us as a farming family was that our farming landscape was degenerating: there were issues with the salinity, water logging, erosion, lack of biodiversity, paddocks being too big, minimal shade and shelter, and lack of ecological balance.

Landcare back in the early 90s was going full steam ahead. There were others in the community that were thinking likewise as a result of the Landcare discussion and networking that had been happening. So the first thing that was done was to get a photo mosaic of the catchment and everyone would then look at their farm on the landscape mosaic and it generated tremendous discussion and interest because we really hadn't seen this sort of thing before.

And then from there strategies were derived and restoration started to occur, identifying the issues, and the solutions, which were common across the landscape. So that over a 20-year period revegetation in this catchment went from 6 per cent to 21 per cent. But it was very much on farmers' and landholders' terms. They were placing trees on landscapes for reasons that mattered to them, and that was really important.

People who had lived in that landscape for many years before and hadn't been there for maybe 10 or 15 years, have been inspired by the significant landscape changes. They talk about the way the landscape has been transformed and 'isn't this great'. There's been a lot of very positive feedback.

We've been involved in family tree-planting projects for 20 years. Each year we have from 20 to 40 people coming from the city – cousins, other relations and their friends – who have become involved in the process, people who have very little exposure to **agriculture**. They just enjoy the experience of coming out and sharing the whole program of revegetating the landscape.

One of the reactions that sticks in my mind is the young girls, who were probably about 20 odd at the time. They came down to help plant some trees on a salt affected area, and then two years later they returned for our annual tree planting time, and the trees had really grown quite well. When we went down there and showed them the trees they planted, they actually started dancing around the trees. They thought it was fantastic.

The real connection between city and country is **food security**. You can see this landscape is actually a place which can produce secure food which can be sustainable. I think our society has this innate perspective about what a good landscape looks like. I notice people – city-based people – can look at this landscape and say, this looks right to me. So that's one of the real motivating things to me: to tap into this innate perspective that people have. When they see a good landscape, they want to be involved in that sort of development.

Andrew Stewart

Source: http://australia21.org.au/reports/repairing-preparing-australias-landscapes-global-change/what-are-the-benefits-and-risks.html

Is revegetation with native species a viable solution to land degradation?

Frayer Graphic Organiser

Handout
ECM 3.5

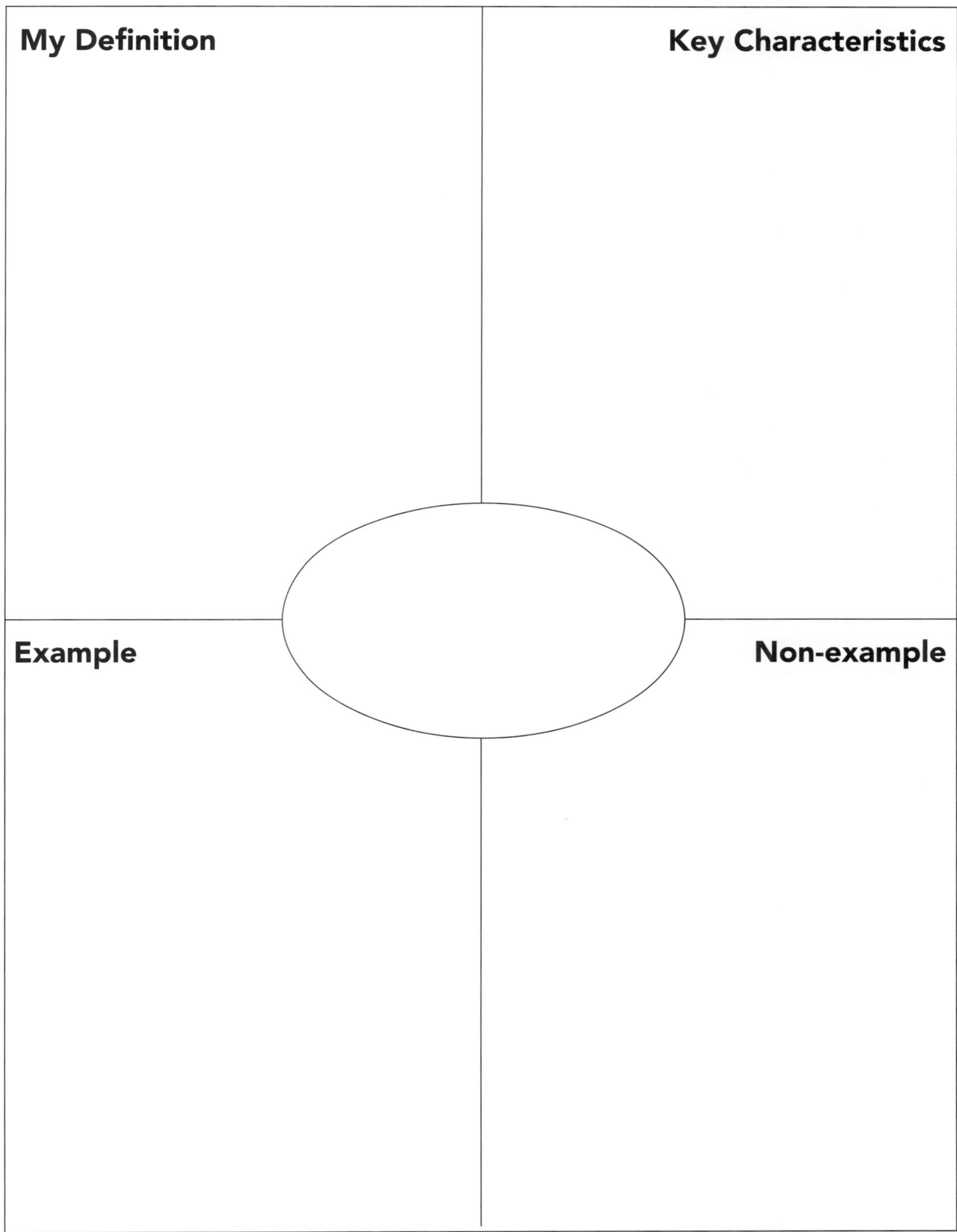

NOTES

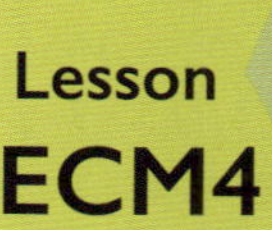

Lesson **ECM4**

ENVIRONMENTAL CHANGE AND MANAGEMENT

How effective is fire as a land management tool?

LEARNING INTENTIONS

- For students to understand the process of **firestick farming** as a way of managing the environment
- For students to evaluate a range of sources for reliability and bias
- For students to draw conclusions from a range of sources

KEY INQUIRY QUESTIONS

- Why is firestick farming used?
- Why is firestick farming an effective land management tool?
- Should firestick farming be more widespread?

KEY VOCABULARY

firestick farming, cultivated

TIME REQUIRED

45 minutes

HANDOUTS

- ECM 4.1 *Dark Emu* synopsis – Firestick farming; one for each student
- ECM 4.2 – Sources (A – E); either a copy of one source for each student, or a whole sheet for each student
- ECM 4.3 – Source Analysis Organiser; one for each student

TEACHER INSTRUCTIONS

PRIOR KNOWLEDGE

No prior knowledge is required for this lesson.

STARTER

1. Provide students with handout ECM 4.1 *Dark Emu* synopsis 'Firestick farming' either prior to the lesson or at the start of the lesson.
2. Show students this video on firestick farming and have them answer the questions below. http://www.abc.net.au/tv/programs/landline/old-site/content/2013/s3767527.htm.

QUESTIONS

a What are the benefits of **controlled burns**?

b Who is Bill Gammage and what is his opinion of fire?

c How has the role of fire in the Australian landscape changed over time?

MAIN ACTIVITY

1. Distribute handout ECM 4.2 'Sources' and handout ECM 4.3 'Source Analysis Organiser'. Students examine the sources and complete the table. When examining the sources for bias, students should look at the author and their motivations for producing the source.

PLENARY

1. Students should then reflect and discuss the following questions (in groups or whole class):
   a) How has the landscape changed since Europeans arrived?
   b) What evidence is there that Australian Aboriginal peoples used fire as a management tool?
   c) Is firestick farming an effective management tool? Should it be more widespread today?
2. Students finish the lesson with a written reflection on firestick farming and environmental management.

DIFFERENTIATION

For less-able students:

- Ask students to complete two or three of the sources – C and D are recommended.

For more-able students:

- Read the links below. Have students assess them for reliability and corroborate them with evidence they have read today.
- http://www.australiangeographic.com.au/news/2010/08/radical-fire-plan-for-the-kimberley
- https://blogs.unimelb.edu.au/sciencecommunication/2014/10/09/fires-with-benefits/
- Students could research the biographies of the authors of the sources to verify if their estimations of reliability are accurate or not.

Dark Emu Synopsis

Handout

ECM 4.1

How effective is fire as a land management tool?

Firestick Farming

The use of fire has always played a central role in Australia's culture. Whilst fire is often viewed in Western society as a threat or danger, Aboriginal Australians hold a very different perspective. Some evidence suggests that Aboriginal Australians began using fire as early as 120,000 years ago. Fire is a tool which, when used responsibly, aids in the creation a landscape that sustains life.

One important way that Aboriginal Australians use fire is a practice called firestick farming. This involves planned and **controlled burns** of lower intensity in order to manage the flora and fauna within a **biome**. This approach to fire worked on five principles:

1. The majority of lands were rotated through in patches or a mosaic pattern, to allow plants and animals to survive in those not being burned.
2. The timing of the fires was adjusted throughout the year, according to the type of country to be burned and the condition that it was already in.
3. The **weather** conditions were strictly considered.
4. Neighbouring clans communicated, advising each other of any fire activity.
5. The burns were not to occur during the growing season of any plants.

Due to this principle of rotation, the land was cultivated into a pattern much like a mosaic, with sections of both cleated land and forest.

Firestick farming provides a method for regulating and managing the natural environment in order to maximise food resources. Better soils were used for food production while the inferior soils were left for forest.

Another important, and possibly more recognised, advantage of firestick farming is the prevention of wildfires.

It's important to recognise that this practice has had a significant impact on Australia's vegetation. Most obviously, Australia's grasslands increased.

Firestick farming is not a practice of the past and still occurs today in some areas.

Source: Adapted from Pascoe, B 2018, Dark Emu, pp. 161–76.

How effective is fire as a land management tool?

Sources

Source A

On the 1 May 1773, English explorer, Captain James Cook, wrote in his diary:

> *Made an excursion into the country which we found diversified with woods, lawns and marshes; the woods are free from underwood of any kind and the trees are at such a distance from one another that the whole country or at least a great part of it might be cultivated without being obliged to cut down a single tree.*
>
> (Cook, J, 1773, Voyages in the Southern Hemisphere)

Source B

Edward Curr, a settler who was born in Hobart, Tasmania in 1820, became a pioneer squatter and knew some of the Aboriginal people who had retained their old culture and values. In the decades of their dispossession he studied them closely, as well as their country. He wrote:

> *... there was another instrument in the hands of these savages which must be credited with results which it would be difficult to over-estimate. I refer to the fire-stick; for the blackfellow was constantly setting fire to the grass and trees ... he tilled his land and cultivated his pastures with fire ...*
>
> (quoted in Gammage, B 2011, p. 185, *The Biggest Estate on Earth*, Allen & Unwin, Sydney)

Source C

This was recounted from the early 1900s by K C Rogers, grazier around Black Mountain:

> *It had been the accepted thing to burn the bush, to provide a new growth of shorter sweet feed for the cattle ... The practice was to burn the country as often as possible, which would be every three or four years according to conditions ... in the hottest and driest weather in January and February, so that the fire would be as hot as possible and thus make a clean burn [but] the long followed practice ... resulted in a great increase of scrub in all the timbered areas.*
>
> (Wakefield, N 1970, p. 153 'Bushfire Frequency and Vegetational Change in SE Australian Forests', *Victorian Naturalist*, No. 87)

Sources

Source D

As at 2018, Tim Flannery is a Professorial Fellow at the Melbourne Sustainable Society Institute, University of Melbourne. He was Chief Commissioner of the **Climate** Commission, a government advisory body, and then formed the Climate Council, an independent climate change organisation. He earned a PhD in Paleontology focusing on *macropods*.

> *As the term firestick farming suggests, the Aboriginal use of fire resembled agriculture in some ways: it yielded certain crops at certain times, suppressed weeds and was carefully controlled ... Aboriginal people are fiercely protective of their clan lands, excluding outsiders or inviting them in as conditions warrant. There are also clear rules about who has the right to what resources and highly evolved mechanisms to resolve conflicts and enforce penalties. This has enabled Australia's Aboriginal people to act as keystone species of the continent's ecosystem for forty-five thousand years. As the Europeans displaced them, Australia's fragile environment collapsed into a far less productive and diverse state.*
>
> (Flannery 2010, p. 100, quoted in Pascoe, Dark Emu, 2012, p. 122).

Source E

Dr Jim Kohen is a lecturer in the School of Biological Sciences at Macquarie University, Sydney.

> *As European settlement spread out from Sydney, traditional Aboriginal burning practices ceased. Once this happened, vegetation associations changed, animals which were once common rapidly declined, and in some cases disappeared altogether. In the more remote areas, this process took longer. In western NSW it happened in the 1840s and 1850s. In parts of Central Australia, the extinctions and declines still continue, although other factors are now involved. However, it can be argued that many of these changes are the result of changed fire regimes. Certainly some of the extinctions of the smaller terrestrial mammals in arid Australia occurred long before the introduction of competitors such as the rabbit and predators like the fox and cat.*
>
> (Kohen, J, The Impact of Fire: An Historical Perspective, paper presented at SGAP Biennial Seminar, 1993)

How effective is fire as a land management tool?

Source Analysis Organiser

Source	What is the main idea of the source?	Is the source reliable? Why/why not?	How does the source link to environmental management?
A			
B			
C			
D			
E			

Lesson **ECM5**

ENVIRONMENTAL CHANGE AND MANAGEMENT

Should Australia diversify its crops?

LEARNING INTENTIONS

- For students to understand **crop diversification** as a solution to land degradation

KEY INQUIRY QUESTIONS

- What **agriculture**/crops does Australia grow?
- What crops did Indigenous Australians grow?
- Should we diversify our agriculture to include some native Australian crops?

KEY VOCABULARY

hunter-gatherer, diversification

TIME REQUIRED

40 mins – 1 hour

HANDOUTS

- ECM 5.1 *Dark Emu* Synopsis – Crop Diversification; one per student
- ECM 5.2 – Mapping Tasks; one per student

TEACHER INSTRUCTIONS

PRIOR KNOWLEDGE

It is expected that students have learnt about:

1. The impact of cattle and sheep on the environment.

STARTER

1. Distribute handout ECM 5.1 *Dark Emu* Synopsis 'Crop Diversification' to students.
2. Have students read the site (could be provided as a print out): https://australianmuseum.net.au/blogpost/science/food-culture-aboriginal-bread.
3. Consider/discuss these questions:
   a. What evidence is there that Aboriginal peoples grew and harvested grain?
   b. What different types of grain did they **harvest**?
   c. How does this challenge the widely accepted view that Aboriginal peoples were **'hunter-gatherers'**?

MAIN ACTIVITY

1. Ask students to complete handout ECM 5.2 'Mapping Tasks'.
2. Discuss as a class: 'Given the fact that the introduction of cattle destroyed many native plants, should we use this area to grow native crops?'

PLENARY

1. Students complete a paragraph on diversifying Australia's crops as a land management technique.

DIFFERENTIATION

For less-able students:

- Have students focus on just one native grain.

For more-able students:

- Students choose one of the news articles below. What implications are there for the future of Australian native crops?
- http://www.abc.net.au/news/rural/2014-05-15/native-australian-wild-rice-indigenous/5455764
- http://www.abc.net.au/news/rural/2017-01-09/potential-for-farmers-to-grow-native-plants/8161212
- http://www.abc.net.au/news/rural/2017-08-30/native-bush-food-demand-outstripping-supply-says-industry/8855058

Should Australia diversify its crops?

Crop Diversification

Handout ECM 5.1

Traditionally grain was grown beyond the high rainfall areas of the coastal regions, while yams were grown in the wetter areas. A wide range of crops were grown, including kangaroo or oat grass, coopers clover, barley grass or native millet (known to Aboriginals as cooly or parpar), and nardoo. Most native Australian grains are naturally gluten-free and don't require chemical supplements for **cultivation.**

People who harvested grain viewed their methods of crop growing as central to their identify and consequently referred to themselves as 'grass people' or 'panara' (Pascoe, 2014 pp. 28).

There is a range of evidence that shows many different stages of **agriculture** including **propagation**, **irrigation**, **harvest** and trade of seed and storage. There is also strong evidence that seeds were domesticated – changed as a result of this agriculture:

> *When plants become 'domesticated' as the result of a human induced selection regime, they undergo changes in the form and structure to such an extent that they often become a new species. Genetic change takes place in this process and the subject plants become dependent on humans for the continuance of their life cycle.* (Gerritsen, R 2008, in Pascoe 2018, p. 39).

Researchers found that some species of native grain developed a tough rachis which can only germinate with artificial watering. Similarly, a bush tomato was discovered to require human intervention to be cultivated.

So what happened to all the native crops? With the colonists came cattle and grazing animals. These animals favoured the native plants and they were quickly lost. Aboriginal peoples consequently lost their sustenance and habitation sites.

A lack of research and general knowledge into, and of, these crops should not be viewed as a lack of evidence, but rather as a result of the disinterest of those who are able to research Aboriginal interaction with the Australian plant communities.

Should Australia diversify its crops?

Revegetation Case Study

Handout **ECM 5.2** (1 of 2)

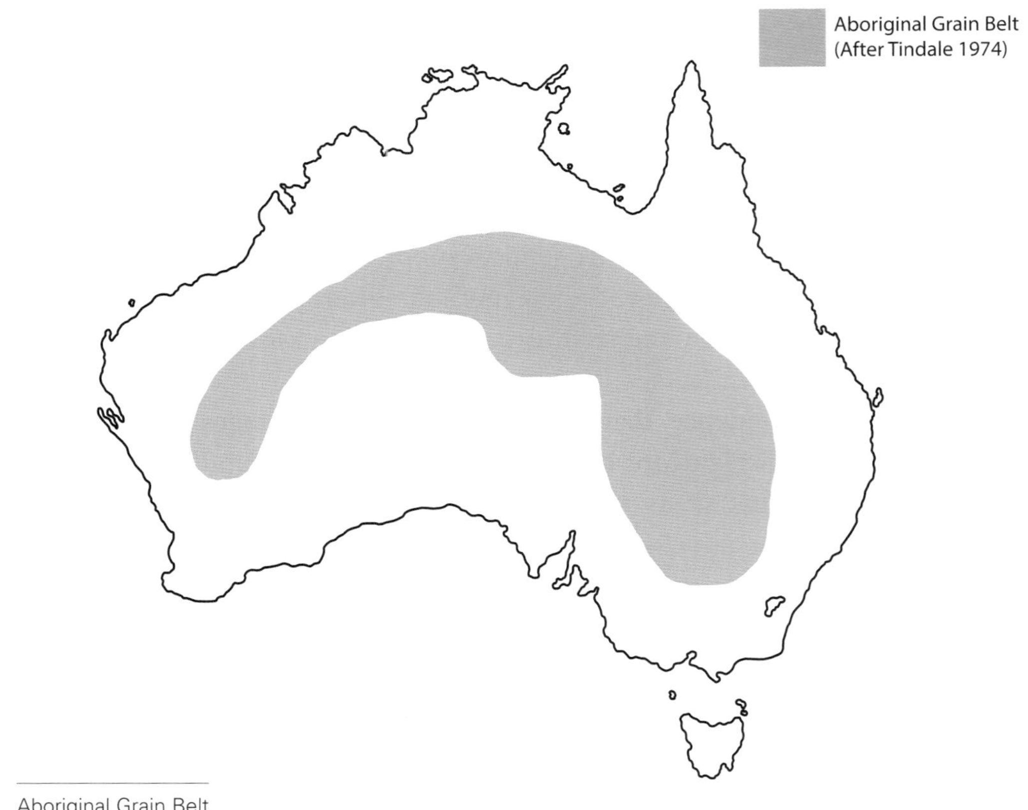

Aboriginal Grain Belt

To view the map detailing Australian land use 2010–11 visit:
http://www.agriculture.gov.au/abares/aclump/land-use

Should Australia diversify its crops?

Mapping Tasks

Source: Adapted from Pascoe, B 2018, Dark Emu, pp.13–67

Compare the two maps – Aboriginal Grain Belt and Australian Land Use 2010–11.

Complete the following:

1. What are the predominant land uses in Australia currently?
2. Estimate the percentage of land of 'grazing native vegetation' and 'minimal use'.
3. Why do you think the land of 'minimal use' is not used for other purposes?
4. What does 'grazing natural vegetation' mean?
5. What impacts do you think 'grazing natural vegetation' would have on the environment?
6. Sketch the Aboriginal grain belt onto the land use map.
7. What is this land currently used for? Identify the four predominant uses.

   Go to: https://public.tableau.com/profile/australian.bureau.of.agricultural.and.resource.economics.and.sci#!/vizhome/Landuseprofiles2017v2/Story

Select a state and region of your choosing:

State: ___________________ Region: ___________________

8. Identify the three main land uses in this area.
9. How do these compare with the predominant land uses in Australia?
10. Identify any areas of the Aboriginal grain belt in this area (note, may not be possible for all regions, you should choose another if it isn't).
11. Given the vast areas that can be used to grow Aboriginal grain, can you identify some areas that could be used accordingly? Use the links below to explore areas where native grains are suitable for growing.

Nardoo (Marsilea drummondi)
http://avh.ala.org.au/occurrences/search?taxa=Marsilea+drummondi#tab_mapView

Pepper grass (Panicum laevinode)
http://avh.ala.org.au/occurrences/search?taxa=Panicum+laevinode#tab_mapView

Native Millet/Barley Grass (Panicum decompositum)
http://avh.ala.org.au/occurrences/search?taxa=Panicum+decompositum#tab_mapView

Coopers Clover (Trigonella sauvissima)
http://avh.ala.org.au/occurrences/search?taxa=Trigonella+suavissima#tab_mapView

NOTES

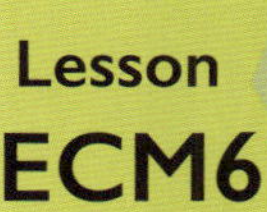

Lesson
ECM6

ENVIRONMENTAL CHANGE AND MANAGEMENT
How should Australia manage its land degradation issues?

LEARNING INTENTIONS

- For students to rank environmental management solutions and justify their decisions

KEY INQUIRY QUESTIONS

- What makes an effective environmental management solution?

KEY VOCABULARY

kangaroo harvesting, firestick farming, crop diversification, revegetation

TIME REQUIRED

20–30 mins

HANDOUTS

- ECM 6.1: Land Management Technique; one per student
- ECM 6.2: Ranking Ladder; one per student

TEACHER INSTRUCTIONS

PRIOR KNOWLEDGE

It is expected that students will have:

1. Completed the activities on firestick farming, **kangaroo harvesting**, **revegetation** and **crop diversification**.

STARTER

1. Ask students to read over their notes on firestick farming, kangaroo harvesting, revegetation and crop diversification.
2. Distribute handout ECM 6.1 'Land Management Techniques' and ask students to complete the table, exploring the advantages and disadvantages of the different solutions.
3. After completing the table, students should compare with a partner and add any missing information.

MAIN ACTIVITY

1. Distribute handout ECM 6.2 'Ranking Ladder'.
2. Using the information in handout ECM 6.1, ask students to rank the solutions from what they believe will be most effective to least effective. They need to be able to justify their decisions.

PLENARY

1. Students then partner up and compare ladders. They discuss and justify, and then decide on a final ranking together. The emphasis of this lesson isn't on a 'right' answer, but students being able to make decisions and justify their opinions.

DIFFERENTIATION

For less-able students:

- Provide these students with one advantage and disadvantage for each topic to get them started.

For more-able students:

- Have students research any other Indigenous land management techniques. Where would they put these on their ladders and why?

Handout ECM 6.1

How should Australia manage its land degradation issues?

Land Management Technique Table

Complete this table of Indigenous land management techniques using your class notes.

Land Management Technique	Advantages	Disadvantages
Kangaroo harvesting		
Firestick farming		
Crop diversification		
Revegetation		

 — ISBN 978 1 925768 64 0 © MAGABALA BOOKS 2019

How should Australia manage its land degradation issues?

Ranking Ladder

Handout
ECM
6.2

Which environmental management technique should we adopt in Australia? Rank the four solutions from what you think would be the most successful, to least successful. Be prepared to be able to justify your decisions.

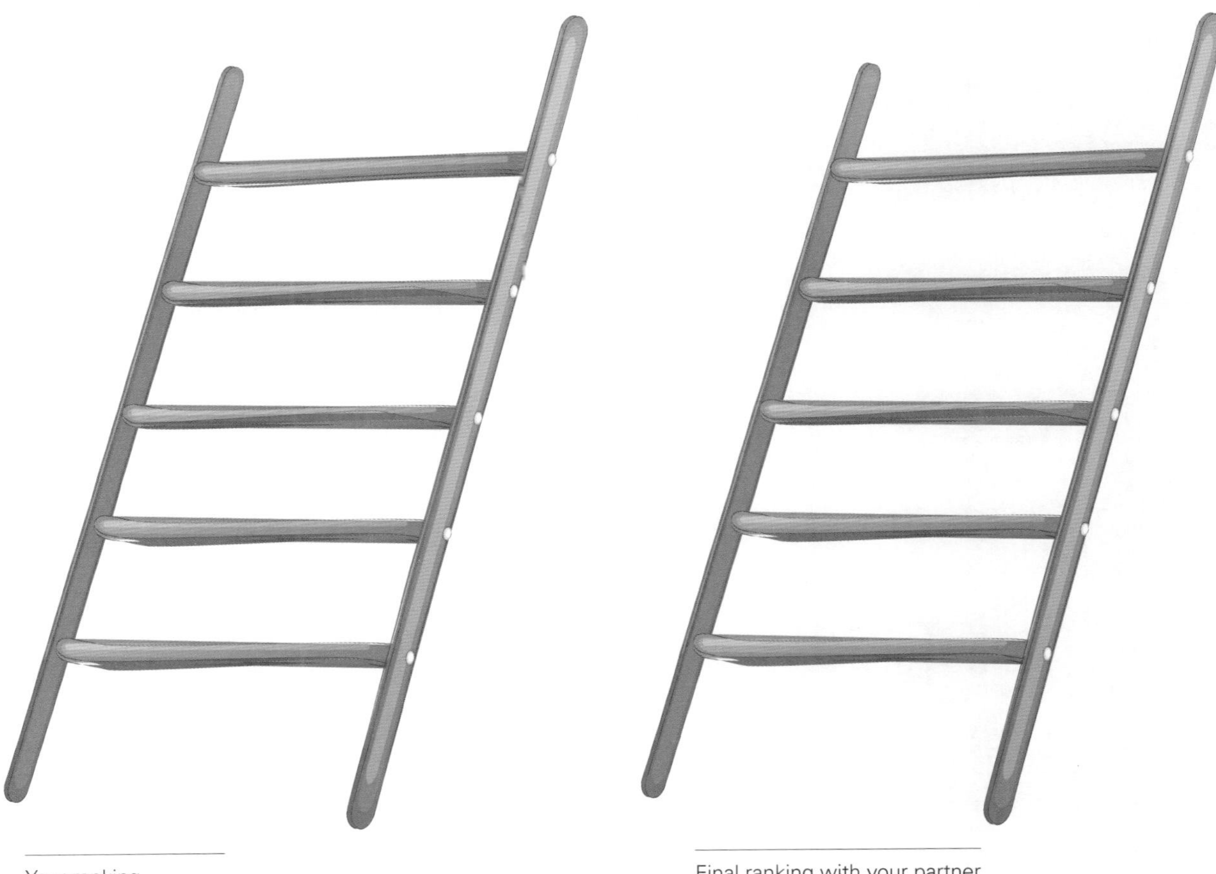

Your ranking

Final ranking with your partner

Compare your ladder with a partner's. How do they compare? Discuss your differences and explain how you decided on your order. As a pair, decide on a final ranking and complete the second ladder.

Lesson RA

REFLECTION ACTIVITY
Where to next?

LEARNING INTENTIONS

- For students to engage in a Socratic discussion, a student-centred formal discussion
- For students to consider the value of Aboriginal and Torres Strait Islander participation in society

KEY INQUIRY QUESTION

- How can Australian society be more inclusive of ATSI peoples and perspectives?

KEY VOCABULARY

colonisation

TIME REQUIRED

45 minutes – 1 hour

HANDOUT

- RA 1 *Dark Emu* Synopsis – The Future; one per student

TEACHER INSTRUCTIONS

PRIOR KNOWLEDGE

It is expected that students have completed some lessons from this *Dark Emu in the Classroom* resource.

STARTER

1. Distribute RA 1 *Dark Emu* Synopsis – The Future.
2. Instruct students to read the synopsis completing the following as they read:
   a. Circle key words.
   b. Underline main ideas.
   c. Put a question mark when there is a term that is not understood.

MAIN ACTIVITY

1. Conduct a discussion using the Socratic method. To do this, begin by arranging students in a circle. You can step out of the circle so that students discuss with each other, rather than using you as mediator.
2. Begin with an open question; it can be generic or tailored to the reading. Here are some examples:
   a. What do you think is the most important key word that you read and why?
   b. What is the main idea in the text?
   c. Which part of the text stands out the most?
   d. Do you feel like you have a voice in society?
   e. What is the value in encouraging ATSI participation in society?
   f. Is the issue of ATSI inclusion easy to answer? Why/why not?
   g. What other issues in society does this link to?

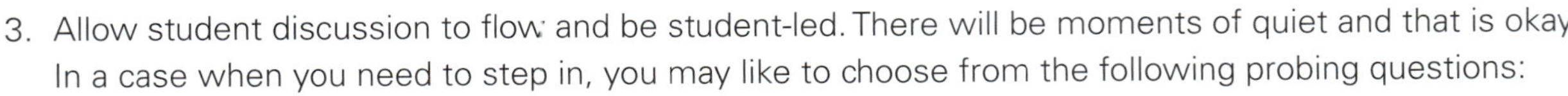

3. Allow student discussion to flow and be student-led. There will be moments of quiet and that is okay. In a case when you need to step in, you may like to choose from the following probing questions:
   a. Taking into account your personal experiences, how did you feel when completing the reading?
   b. As a young person, what do you think you could do to encourage Aboriginal participation?
   c. Who has a different opinion?

PLENARY

1. As discussion comes to a natural close, thank students for their participation. Ask students to write a short reflection.

DIFFERENTIATION

For less-able students:

- You may create a second circle of observers partnered up with one student from the inner circle. You may provide them with a graphic organiser to fill in, monitoring their partner's activity and reflecting on the most interesting point their partner made. They can share their reflections at the end.

For more-able students:

- You may pair this with an extra reading. Two recommended articles: Arrente woman and feminist Celeste Liddle's piece on reconciliation available at http://www.dailylife.com.au/news-and-views/dl-opinion/reconciliation-shouldnt-just-be-driven-by-indigenous-people-20150525-gh9eh9.html or Darkinjung Aboriginal Land Council CEO Sean Gordon's available at https://nit.com.au/exclusive-turnbull-stuffed-2017-says-gordon/.

SUGGESTED ADAPTATIONS

Provide the reading before class to be completed for homework.

If you wish for a more formal discussion procedure, this may assist you: https://www.facinghistory.org/resource-library/teaching-strategies/socratic-seminar.

Dark Emu Synopsis

Where to next?

The Future

Handout
ECM RA1

It is often said that history is written by the victors. In the case of Australia, much of the narrative of this country's past was created by early European colonists and repeated over subsequent decades by their children and grandchildren. It was common for European colonists in Australia to ignore, or even destroy, the society of the land's existing inhabitants. This was done by downplaying the complexity and depth of Aboriginal Australians' connections to their land, and by denying their humanity. Often it was done by brutal violence and murder. But by writing the experience and knowledge of Aboriginal Australians out of the story of modern Australia, we have lost 'those elements – like the crops, houses, **irrigation** systems and fisheries [that] may hold keys to future prosperity' (Pascoe B 2018, p. 224).

The story of human evolution is often told from one of two points of view. The first says that only the fittest survive; life is a fierce competition in which the weakest individuals – and civilisations – eventually die. This is a view that fits well with the history written by European colonists. It also matches modern economic and political approaches that emphasise capitalism, private business and rapid technological progress. But others suggest that human history has always been marked by a degree of cooperation with, and care for, other humans and the natural environment. The survival of individuals depends on the survival of the human species and the preservation of the planet. This idea aligns more closely with Aboriginal Australian spiritual systems, cultural practices and ways of living prior to **colonisation**, but may also be of value to us today. Modern economic systems often prioritise profit and progress over the protection of air quality, land or clean water.

Rediscovering, celebrating and learning from Aboriginal stories, experience and achievements is an important part of addressing Australia's colonial past, for both Aboriginal and non-Aboriginal Australians. By meaningfully including Aboriginal Australians and their history in the history of Australia, and by fully involving them in Australia's future, we might go some way toward reducing the continuing damage of colonialism. This is not a simple task, but we can begin by acknowledging that Aboriginal Australians built houses, cultivated and irrigated crops and sewed clothes. Over many thousands of years Aboriginal Australians learnt how to increase the productivity of the land and this enormous expertise is useful to us today.

Source: Pascoe 2018, pp. 218–29

Teacher Resource I

KEY VOCABULARY LIST

aeration	The process of puncturing the soil in order to improve water drainage and improve the uptake of nutrients by crops.
agriculture	The cultivation of land – including growing crops and breeding animals – to produce food and other products that sustain life.
aquaculture	The cultivation of the sea or inland waters to produce food.
biome	A large ecological community of plants and animals that are adapted to a particular climate or environment and that share an extended geographical area – terrestrial biomes are those on land, aquatic biomes are those in water.
climate	The general and recurring weather conditions of a particular area – including rainfall, temperature, air pressure, humidity and sunshine.
colonisation	The process by which a group of people establish themselves outside their native country and assume control of the Indigenous people.
controlled burns	The use of fire under specific conditions and at a planned time to clear land, reduce the danger of bushfire, or to promote the regrowth of vegetation.
crop diversification	The deliberate cultivation of different crops in order to reduce the danger of food shortages caused by poor harvests.
cropping	The planting of particular food, fibre or medicinal crops.
cultivation	The use of labour or machinery to promote or improve the growth of crops.
dyke	An embankment or structure designed to restrain or direct the flow of water.
ecosystem	A community of organisms that interact with one another and with their shared environment.
firestick farming	The use of controlled burning by Aboriginal Australians to facilitate hunting and to promote the growth of vegetation.
food insecurity	The state of being without reliable access to a sufficient quantity of affordable, nutritious food.
food security	The secure access to adequate food to meet the needs of a healthy population.
hard-hooved	A description of animals – such as cows or horses – whose feet can cause significant damage to vulnerable environments and vegetation.
harvest	To gather the products of cropping or other agricultural processes.
hunter-gatherer	An individual or society that survives wholly or primarily on food that is collected or hunted in the natural environment.

Teacher Resource I (CONT.)

KEY VOCABULARY LIST

irrigation	The planned diversion of water to specific areas to promote the growth of crops or the sustenance of animals.
kangaroo harvesting	The commercial hunting of wild kangaroos.
macropods	Plant-eating marsupials of Australia, including the kangaroo.
overfishing	The removal of fish from waters at a greater rate than breeding can replace.
pasture	An area of ground covered by grass used or suitable for the grazing of cattle.
propagation	The process of causing plants or animals to reproduce and increase in number.
quota	A limit applied to the number of animals hunted in order to maintain their populations.
revegetation	The purposeful planting of native plant species to rehabilitate degraded land.
rom	Law or culture according to the *Yolngu* language group of Arnhem Land.
saltwater intrusion	The increase in soil salinity caused by the destruction of native vegetation and the subsequent degradation of land.
spatial distribution	The spread of particular features or phenomena across the earth's surface.
staple crop	A particular crop that forms the primary source of cultivated food for a population.
sustainability	The maintenance of resources to meet the needs of current populations without compromising the needs of future generations.
terra nullius	Latin term translating to 'land belonging to no one' used by European colonists to validate colonisation.
terracing	The planting of crops on hillside steps, which prevents valuable nutrients from being washed away with rain.
terrestrial biomes	A large ecological community of land plants and animals that are adapted to a particular climate or environment and that share an extended geographical area.
tuber	An enlarged structure of some plant species that stores nutrients, and which is often used by people as a food source – for example potatoes and yams.
weather	The state of the atmosphere at a particular time and place with respect to rainfall, temperature, air pressure, humidity and sunshine.

Teacher Resource 2

VOCABULARY ACTIVITIES

The aim of these activities is for students to understand key terminology used in the unit. For the terms and definitions used in the activities, see the key vocabulary provided.

1. **Find your buddy:** Print the key vocabulary and choose enough definitions for half the class. Cut up, making sure you separate term and definition. Provide each student with one slip of paper – either a term or definition. Have students move around the room and find their partner, i.e. if there are 24 students in your class, choose 12 terms and definitions and cut them up.
2. **Bluff:** For unfamiliar terms, provide three definitions – one true and two false. Have students work in pairs to decide which is accurate.
3. **Pictionary:** Chose a student to or simply draw the term on the whiteboard. This can also be played in small teams with more familiar words.
4. **Mix and match:** Mix up the terms and definitions and have students match them.
5. **Heads and hips:** Create true/false statements based on the key terms and play heads or hips. Read out a statement (e.g. Agriculture refers to the growing of crops) and students choose if it's true or false by putting their hands on their heads or hips (while standing). Last person standing wins.
6. **Circle race:** Divide students into two teams each sitting in a circle on chairs. Read out a statement (e.g. Agriculture refers to the growing of crops) and students choose if it's true or false by moving one seat to the left (true) or to the right (false). The first team seated to have moved in the correct direction receives a point.
7. **Bingo:** Students select nine key words and put them into a 3x3 grid – one in each box. Teacher reads aloud the definitions only, and students guess the term and cross it out if they have it. Play with different levels of difficulty – outside corners, rows, or blackout.
8. **Flashcard quiz:** Key terms are printed onto small cards, one set per team. Students work in pairs and play against one other pair, taking it in turns. One student chooses a random card from the top of the pile, and chooses three words (other than the term) as hints to their partner. Their partner needs to guess the term. For example, if the word is 'climate' the student may say 'weather over time' and the partner has to guess. One point is awarded for every correct guess, and each team gets one minute to get as many as possible. It's important the other team pays attention. Teams swap and the other team has a turn (same set of cards). Teams keep swapping one-minute turns until all the cards are used.